DIVORCE IS EXPENSIVE

8 REMEDIAL SECTIONS FOR THE CONFLICTING COUPLES

DIVORCE IS EXPENSIVE

8 REMEDIAL SECTIONS FOR THE CONFLICTING COUPLES

Authored By,

C Shankary B.A., LLB.

ADVOCATE, MADRAS HIGH COURT, 9962819832

PARTNERED WITH M/S. NATHAN AND ASSOCIATES, CHENNAI.

TLC MASTERMINDS PUBLISHING

Office Address- No. 16, 3rd Main Road, Jaganathapuram,
Velachery, Chennai 600042 (TN) India

Website: https://www.tlcpublishing.org/
Email: info.tlcpublishing@gmail.com

Published by TLC Publishing International 2025
Title : DIVORCE IS EXPENSIVE
Price : Rs.499 | $9
ISBN : 978-93-6006-040-4

ACKNOWLEDGMENTS AND DEDICATIONS

There are numerous reasons why books must be published and one of the reasons that I have is to make the readers aware of the procedures and functioning of the Laws of the Indian Courts. The book will have in depth knowledge about the Laws especially the Family Law giving readers insights before taking a big decision in life. Additionally this book will help the readers to understand the rich history and culture of our country.

First and foremost, I wish to dedicate this book to the Almighty Shiradi Sai Baba, who has blessed me to become an Author. In the loving memory of my grandmother, Kamala Amma, who instilled a fearless spirit inside me through her unwavering blessings throughout my life. I dedicate this book to the cherished memory of my father, Shri G. Chandrasekaran, who passed away at the age of 48. His interactions within our joint family and his relationships with friends and well-wishers imparted invaluable lessons to me. I often wonder if there exists another individual so universally loved and esteemed as a true Paragon.

I wish to express my heartfelt gratitude to my mother,

Mrs. Suguna Chandrasekaran, who, despite having only an 8th-grade education, aspired for all three of her children to become professionally qualified. Today, I have elevated myself to the role of a Thought Leader. It was her vision that led me to pursue a career as an advocate. I am deeply grateful to my brother, Mr. Sarvanan, and my sister, Mrs. Manogary, for their unwavering support. Their constant encouragement and belief in me, expressed through their words, ***"You can do it,"*** continue to inspire and motivate me.

I am deeply grateful to my husband, Mr. B.N. Perumal Raja, who constantly encourages me to reach for the stars. He is my greatest inspiration, my best friend, and my strongest pillar of support. I also wish to thank my son, Master R. Sai Sanjay, the light of my life and the very essence of my heart, living outside my body.

I extend my heartfelt gratitude to all my in-laws, especially my mother-in-law, Mrs. Navaneetham Balan, my father-in-law, Mr. K. Balan, and my brother-in-law, Mr. Suresh, whose unwavering belief in me has never wavered.

I thank my aunts, Dr. Aruna Singh, Mrs. Komala Prebagar, and Mrs. Sudharsana Anand, along with all my cousin brothers and sisters, whose genuine happiness for even my smallest successes has always meant so much to me.

I sincerely thank my senior, Shri P.S. Jagannathan, for illuminating my path in this noble profession. As a first-generation advocate, I was fortunate to receive his invaluable guidance, which paved the way for many empanelments to come automatically due to my association as his junior.

I am deeply indebted to the following individuals who helped me recognize my true potential: Mr. N.V.A. Madhavan, Mr. S. Ruban Prabhu, Mrs. B.S. Ajeetha, Mrs. Sudha Ramalingam, Ms. S.P.Arthi, Mr. Sunil Sethia, Mr. Ajeeth Nager, Mrs. Sujatha V. Hari, Mrs. B.S. Prapoorna, Mr. M.R. Krishnan, Mr. Muzzammil Altaf, Mr. Murali Sundaram, Mr. Kaviyanathan. D.O., and Mrs. Niveditha Kaviyanathan. Their guidance and support have been invaluable on my journey.

I wish to express my gratitude and give due credit to my Juniors, Mrs. S. Vijayalakshmi and Ms. Neerraja Kannan, as well as my advocate friend, Mrs. S. M. Umayal, for their invaluable assistance in completing this book. And also thank each and every human being who helps me learn and develop each and everyday in my life.

Table of Content

Foreword

The author of this book titled "Divorce is Expensive" is an advocate who has been known to me for the past 20 years. She has been a consistently practicing lawyer for 25 years. In the times when women lawyers faced several hurdles in the field of litigation practice, she stepped into the bar as a lawyer and has been in regular practice to date. Once a woman becomes a lawyer, it is a herculean task to find a senior to learn and look forward for mentoring. To sustain the practice of law from on her own for 25 years is nothing short of an achievement. I warmly congratulate the author, Mrs. C. Shankary, for the same.

"Ignorance of Law is no excuse" is a legal maxim that is per force cast upon any individual in our Democratic Republic. But the reality is otherwise. It is an undeniable truth that even though a person is educated, well - read and holding a good position in any other field, they could still be a legally illiterate. So they would wish to know the provisions of law on marriage, divorce and other related rights when it becomes necessary for them. These aspects of legal remedies are not taught anywhere except at law schools. Hence, the contents of the book are relevant for every household that is exposed to any matrimonial turbulence either for themselves or for their near and dear ones. It is with surprise I have noted in my personal experience that even educated men and women are ignorant about the laws and the ways in which laws can be used as tools.

In the present days of enhanced women's independence, especially financially, though not to the extent desirable and required, women are equally thrust into multi-tasking in different ways as compared to, say, a hundred years ago. The women are the axis of the family and are now made to face different challenges at home. With the enactment of Legislations like the Protection of Women from Domestic Violence Act, 2005, Sexual Harassment of Women at Workplace (Prevention, Prohibition, and Redressal) Act, 2013 and amendments to other laws like the Maternity Benefit Act, women are sought to be more empowered. These positive steps have led to a more assertive woman who does not hesitate from seeking legal remedies available for the myriad disputes on the matrimonial front. It is in this context that this book, written in simple and straightforward narrative, will help to fill the void in the assistance of men and women in the path to resolving their marital disputes within the framework of law. The book's title is sure to kindle the curiosity of anyone to get the book and read, even if one is a lawyer.

This book not only explains the legal provisions of Hindu Marriage Act, 1955 but also gives the equivalent and corresponding provisions of other personal laws governing Christians, Parsis and the persons of inter faith married under the Special Marriage Act.

However, the Muslim Divorce Law is not included in the Tabular Column and finds less mention in the book.

This book will be useful for the persons who look forward to know about the broader outlines and finer details about various options at hand to deal with any matrimonial problem. The Book has painted the Divorce landscape of our country for the reader and filled with details and narratives of various remedies such as divorce, judicial separation, restitution of conjugal rights, interim maintenance and permanent alimony, custody and maintenance for minor children, return of Sridham articles, etc. The highlight is the author's explanations and experiences, which make the reading more interesting.

On the whole, this book would be useful for anyone who looks forward to know various options before they decide to proceed in the court of law. It is as informative as one would get from a Matrimonial cases lawyer. The persons who need awareness would benefit the most from this book.

Though it is a maiden effort of the author, she has done a commendable job in attempting a book about a very vast subject in an abridged form, which adds to the readability of the book.

No book can be complete in its content, as there is an ocean of information to be conveyed. Even these days, AI - powered search engines are available on any subject and especially law and procedure they, are in abundance. Shifting the required and relevant information is an uphill task that one may not succeed all the time. But this book is informative. And still, it is a pleasure reading books in spite of the swarm of digital books and materials that are available.

It will not be complete if I fail to express my doubts about certain views of the author based on her personal beliefs and ideology to which I do not subscribe, as it is beyond the legal rights that are enshrined in various laws. I leave it to the readers to reflect upon such opinions of the author. Having said that, I record my appreciation that the book is very informative on legal aspects of divorce of persons belonging to various personal laws in our society, who may not be aware of the intricacies of the laws on Marriage and Divorce.

The benefit of reading this book is that it throws light on the subject and protects one from believing anyone blindly. This book helps the innocent and ignorant litigant to make decisions upon informed choices available for both the parties before availing legal services to obtain legal remedies from courts of law to get justice and live their life with contentment.

Date: 18.03.2025,
Chennai.

B. S. AJEETHA
ADVOCATE.

Foreword

"Divorce" is the legal process of dissolving the marital bond between the couple, which often includes the division of assets, child custody, and spousal support. In other words, it is an official termination of a marriage through due process of law; it signifies the end of legal obligations and responsibilities associated with marriage.

However, in view of a drastic change in living conditions and a change in social environment, the sacrament and sanctity of marriage are diminishing and lost. Divorce cases are mounting throughout the country, influenced by shifting societal attitudes. The attitudes of the parties before the Family Court and District Court, were completely changed and they approached the Court by way of procuring their daily needs in a mall and multi-store.

Some people find that divorce allows them to move forward and pursue a happier and more independent life and, on some occasions, it leads to financial benefits for one or both parties. While, so in certain circumstances, either it can provide a healthy environment or remove dysfunctional households.

The concept of Divorce was not originally recognized, as marriage was considered a sacred and unbreakable bond. In Hinduism, there was no provision's earlier for divorce until the introduction of Hindu Marriage Act, 1955. Under this

Act, divorce is allowed under specific circumstances such as cruelty, desertion, or mutual consent. The Act promulgates the legal process for dissolving marriage through the court system. Similarly, various other laws were enacted for the dissolution of marriages performed in other religions and inter-caste marriages viz., Special Marriage Act and Indian Divorce Act.

The author of this book does a commendable job in bringing out this book with her own experiences gained in her professional life and cited relevant case laws. The author's view is a valuable exploration of her distinguished career. I am confident that this book will serve as a valuable resource for those engaged in the legal profession and a must-read for young lawyers eager to understand the path forward in respect of filing cases dissolving the marriage in accordance with Law and its significance.

A. PRABHAKARAN,
ADVOCATE.

CHAPTER 1

INTRODUCTION

CHAPTER 1

DIVORCE IS EXPENSIVE

8 REMEDIAL SECTIONS FOR THE CONFLICTING COUPLES

INTRODUCTION:

Dear Readers, Advocate Friends, Respected Seniors, and Energetic Juniors, I am delighted to present my 25 years of practical experience in courts for the benefit of the greater good. I am publishing this book with a huge hope that I am giving my best and 10x value through this book. This book will explain to you the functioning of Indian courts in personal laws. I have thoroughly examined the Hindu Marriage Act of 1955, focusing on its various sections. All the personal laws related to other religions bear similarities to the Hindu Marriage Act of 1955. Only minor additions based on the customs of other religions will be made to the other personal laws. I have also given a tabular column in the last chapter before the conclusion for comparison and easy understanding. **"LAW IS NOTHING BUT A COMMON MAN'S UNDERSTANDING."** This book helps you understand the basic architecture of the Act and the forward thinking of the drafting committee of the personal laws of each and every religion in our country. The existing personal laws cover every Indian citizen.

History is always important to know from which origin and culture we have come. And also, to understand whether we have lost our standard of thinking or improved our thoughts in this fast world. This book will educate you on court procedures, and

I have shared the cases I have handled and how I have helped my clients get their rightful remedies using the latest amendments of this Act, which will help people in mental agony, pain, and suffering. Unlike other litigations, this relationship problem between a married couple is more of an emotional involvement; the trust, belief, and feeling in the other partner are shattered.

In life, we focus on three major aspects: health, wealth, and relationships. Two other factors interconnect this relationship. Individuals grappling with personal issues often experience both indirect and direct losses in their health and wealth. They will spend all their valuable time thinking about the positive aspects of their partner and shall have a fond hope that they will rejoin the matrimonial life on the one hand. And the other type of person thinks about the bad aspects of their partner and will always be in the mood to get away from this marriage. It involves lots of other aspects, like influencers in the family, friends, and general ideas they read and hear from the people who come for their case. However, it is often misunderstood that each individual's life problem is unique, leading to varying outcomes.

HISTORY OF THE EMERGENCE OF THIS ACT

Before we talk about any act, we should know its reasons and objectives. Only then can we understand the culture and identify the fundamental rights of the Constitution that have been violated and the new law that evolved to protect them. Likewise, Articles 13(3), 19, and 21 of our Constitution were affected by personal laws. The law is meant to treat all people equally, and it is the state's responsibility to protect every single one of its citizens.

1. Article 13 of the Constitution of India

Article 13 of the Indian Constitution deals with laws that contradict or violate fundamental rights.

2. Article 13(3) of the Constitution

"Law" in this article includes any ordinance, order, bye-law, rule, regulation, notification, custom, or usage that has the force of law in India, unless the context states otherwise.

Key Points of Article 13

1. Laws inconsistent with fundamental rights are void.
2. The state cannot make laws that take away or abridge fundamental rights.
3. The article defines "law" to include additional fractions of laws and regulations.
4. This article does not apply to the amendments under Article 368.

Article 13 of the Constitution of India: An Analysis

1. Article 13 prohibits laws from violating fundamental rights.
2. The Article restricts the state from introducing laws that impact basic rights.
3. Article 13 provides for judicial review of laws, enabling courts to invalidate them, allowing judges to strike down laws that violate fundamental rights.

3. Article 19(1)(e) of the Constitution of India

Freedom to Live and Settle:

Article 19(1)(e) assures one of the freedom to live and settle anywhere in India. People are free to decide where they live and settle anywhere around the nation. However, we can place reasonable limitations on this right to maintain public order, safeguard scheduled tribes, or uphold India's sovereignty and integrity.

In the case of [1]***U.P. Avas Evam Vikas Parishad v. Friends Co-op. Housing Society Ltd. (1995),*** the Supreme Court said that the right to live includes the right to a house or the right to reside, which is protected by Article 19(1)(e). This includes the right to reside, the right to shelter, or the right to build houses for that purpose.

4. Article 21 of the Constitution of India

Personal liberty and the protection of life

None will be denied his life or personal liberty except in accordance with legal procedures.

Author's explanation:

Article 21 of the Indian Constitution says that everyone has the right to protect their life and personal freedom. It provides certain safeguards against the unjustifiable denial of freedom and life.

[1] - Sourced from indiakanoon.org

Article 21 states that only the legal process can take away someone's life. In this way, everyone has the right to live, and their life can only be taken away by following the steps set out by law. Article 21 stresses the right to a healthy environment, the right to a decent life, and the right to be able to make a living.

Freedom of choice is also protected by Article 21. This law asserts that it cannot deny anyone their personal freedom unless it explicitly states so. Some other things that make up personal liberty are the freedom to go and live wherever you want and the ability to work legally at any job.

In the landmark case [2]***A.K. Gopalan v. The State of Madras,*** the Supreme Court said that personal liberty means "liberty of the body," which means not being arrested or jailed for no reason. The Supreme Court also said that the word "law" only refers to state-made laws. In later cases, though, the judiciary changed this point of view.

In the case of [3]***R.C. Cooper v. Union of India (1970),*** the court ruled that the phrase "personal liberty" would include both Article 21 and the six Fundamental Freedoms set out in Article 19(1). So, Article 21 speaks of both freedom and rights.

According to the decision in [4]***Kharak Singh v. State of Uttar Pradesh, AIR 1963,*** the court ruled that "personal liberty" would mean more than just the rights set out in Article 19(1).

[2] - Sourced from indiakanoon.org
[3] - Sourced from indiakanoon.org
[4] - Sourced from indiakanoon.org

In the landmark case of [5]***Maneka Gandhi v. Union of India (1978),*** the Supreme Court said in Article 21 that the right to life and personal liberty is not only a right but also a right to live with respect. The court made it clear that the new legal system must be fair, just, and logical; it can't be random, harsh, or irrational.

In [6]***Olga Tellis v. Bombay Municipal Corporation (1985),*** the court accepted that the right to a living was an important part of the right to life under Article 21. The court was right when it said that people living on the pavement would be violating their rights to life and personal freedom if they were evicted without being given a new place to live.

In the landmark case [7]***Vishaka v. State of Rajasthan (1997),*** the Supreme Court dealt with the issue of sexual abuse at work. The court ruled that making sure workers are safe and secure at work is a fundamental right that comes from Article 21. The court established guidelines to prevent and address sexual harassment in the workplace, pending the enactment of appropriate laws.

The National Legal Services Authority filed a PIL in [8]***National Legal Services Authority v. Union of India and Ors. (2014)*** to defend the rights of transgender people. When the court examined the Right to Life Article, it decided that a person's gender should be based on who they are. So, transgender people should have all the rights that regular people do, like using public bathrooms and getting medical care. They should also be

[5] - Sourced from indiakanoon.org
[6] - Sourced from indiakanoon.org
[7] - Sourced from indiakanoon.org
[8] - Sourced from indiakanoon.org

able to use the reservations in Articles 15 and 16 because they are a minority group.

In the landmark case of [9]***K.S. Puttaswamy v. Union of India (2017)*** (Right to Privacy Decision), the Supreme Court recognized that Article 21 protects the basic right to privacy. The court came to the conclusion that privacy is incorporated into the Constitution and is an important part of human freedom and dignity.

The right to die with respect was acknowledged as a basic right by the court in [10]***Common Cause v. Union of India (2018),*** which was based on Article 21. The court said that people can refuse medical care or life support and can write down their wishes in advance if they are diagnosed with a fatal illness.

Furthermore, Article 21 states that arbitrary or illegal arrest is not allowed. This law says that no one can be jailed without sufficient cause or without following the rules of due process. It prevents unjustified detention and unlawful deprivation of freedom. It also talks about the right to a fair hearing. It makes sure that everyone who is accused of a crime has the right to a fair trial, including the right to a lawyer, a hearing, and the chance to show evidence in their defence.

Because of this, Article 21's meaning and scope have changed over the course of several landmark decisions of the Supreme Court. It now includes protection against torture and attack in prison, and the right to a clean and healthy environment. So, the freedoms guaranteed by Article 21 can be limited in ways

[9] - Sourced from indiakanoon.org
[10] - Sourced from indiakanoon.org

that are fair for the sake of public order, national security, public health, or morality. Still, these restrictions must be fair, sensible, and in line with what is reasonable and right.

This article by itself has been thoroughly discussed, as the readers should grasp people's rights and freedom in order to treat other human beings with dignity.

Separation or divorce did not exist before 1955. Men led their lives as they pleased. Women had neither voice nor choice. The primary man behind this act was Dr B.R. Ambedkar. It is encouraging that the Hindu Code Bill has reforms brought about by law. A formal break in marriage approved by the court, known as judicial separation, could later become a patch-up between the pair. The court's aim in allowing the aggrieved party relief from judicial separation is to evaluate their relationship and provide another opportunity before divorce.

India is a democratic nation; hence it has numerous laws controlling several kinds of marriages and supporting the rights and responsibilities of married couples. Here are some of the main marriage laws in India together with their Objectives and Reasons:

The Hindu Marriage Act, 1955

Objectives:

1. The primary objective is to codify Hindu marriage law, which will provide a comprehensive and uniform legal framework for Hindu marriages.
2. The second objective is to prohibit practices such as polygamy,

child marriage (below 15 years) , and forced marriage.

3. The third objective is to provide for divorce and the rights and obligations of spouses.

Reasons:

1. The need to reform and codify Hindu marriage law, which was previously governed by various customs and traditions.
2. The second goal is to promote monogamy and prohibit polygamy.
3. To protect the rights of Hindu women and provide them with greater autonomy and equality,

Muslim Personal Law (Shariat) Application Act, 1937

Objectives:

1. Apply Shariat law to Muslims in India, consequently governing their personal law, including marriage.
2. The second objective is to regulate divorce and the rights and obligations of spouses.

Reasons:

1. The need to provide a uniform and comprehensive law governing Muslim personal law, including marriage.
2. To protect the rights of Muslim women and provide them with greater autonomy and equality.
3. The third reason is to promote social reform and modernization within the Muslim community.

Special Marriage Act, 1954

Objectives

1. The primary objective is to facilitate marriages between individuals of different faiths and castes.
2. To provide for civil marriages, which are not governed by personal law.
3. The third objective is to promote secularism and the principles of equality and justice.

Reasons:

1. The need to provide a secular law governing marriages, which would apply to all citizens regardless of their faith or caste.
2. The second reason is to promote national integration and unity by providing a common law governing marriages.
3. The third reason is to protect the individual rights and freedoms of citizens, including the right to choose their partner and marry outside their faith or caste.

Parsi Marriage and Divorce Act, 1936

Objectives:

1. The aim is to provide a comprehensive law that governs Parsi marriages and divorces.
2. The second objective is to regulate the registration of Parsi marriages.
3. The third objective is to provide for divorce and the rights and obligations of spouses.

Reasons

1. The need to codify and provide a comprehensive law governing Parsi marriages and divorce.
2. The second reason is to protect the rights of Parsi women and provide them greater autonomy and equality.
3. The third reason is to promote social reform and modernization within the Parsi community.

Indian Christian Marriage Act, 1872

Objectives:

1. The aim is to provide a comprehensive law governing Christian marriages.
2. The second objective is to regulate the registration of Christian marriages.
3. The third objective is to provide for divorce and the rights and obligations of spouses.

Reasons:

1. The need to codify and provide a comprehensive law governing Christian marriages.
2. The second reason is to protect the rights of Christian women and provide them greater autonomy and equality.
3. The third reason is to promote social reform and modernization within the Christian community.

Key Takeaways of all Personal Laws:

1. The Act defines marriage as a sacrament and a union between two persons.
2. The Act specifies conditions for a valid marriage, including the age of the parties, mental capacity, and prohibited relationships.
3. The Act promotes monogamy by prohibiting bigamy and polygamy.
4. The Act provides for divorce on various grounds, including adultery, desertion, and cruelty.
5. The Act provides for maintenance of the wife or husband and children in case of divorce or separation.
6. The Act grants property rights to the wife and children in case of divorce or separation.

Impact and significance:

1. The Act reformed law by providing a uniform and comprehensive code governing marriages.
2. The Act protected women's rights by promoting monogamy, providing for divorce, and granting property rights.
3. The Act promoted social reform by prohibiting practices like bigamy and polygamy.
4. The Act has led to numerous judicial precedents, shaping the interpretation and application of marriage law.

CHAPTER 2

D- DIVORCE BY MUTUAL CONSENT

Section 13-B of the Hindu Marriage Act, 1955, says:

13-B Divorce by Mutual Consent.

(1) Subject to the provisions of this Act, a petition for dissolution of marriage by a decree of divorce may be presented to the district court by both the parties to a marriage together, whether such marriage was solemnized before or after the commencement of the Marriage Laws (Amendment) Act, 1976 (68 of 1976), on the ground that they have been living separately for a period of one year or more, that they have not been able to live together, and that they have mutually agreed that the marriage should be dissolved.

(2) On the motion of both the parties made not earlier than six months after the date of the presentation of the petition referred to in sub-section (1) and not later than eighteen months after the said date, if the petition is not withdrawn in the meantime, the court shall, on being satisfied, after hearing the parties and after making such inquiry as it thinks fit, that a marriage has been solemnized and that the averments in the petition are true, pass a decree of divorce declaring the marriage to be dissolved with effect from the date of the decree.

AUTHOR'S EXPLANATION:

By mutual consent, the parties to the marriage separate by their voluntary consent after understanding their differences of opinion, realizing they cannot live together without disturbing each other's mental peace, and realizing they cannot make the dead marriage work. And the biggest privilege is that they need not express the fault of each other in papers but simply express that the marriage has been irretrievably broken.

Both parties to a marriage must petition the appropriate court for a decree of divorce on the grounds that they have been living separately for one year or more, have been unable to live together as husband and wife, and have mutually agreed to dissolve the marriage.

On presentation of the petition by both parties, the waiting period is six months and can be extended to eighteen months and not more than that period. As long as the parties to the marriage don't withdraw their petition, the court will declare the marriage over as soon as it is satisfied that the petitioners' claims that they were married and that the marriage ended are true. This will happen after hearing from both sides of the marriage and any other inquiries the court deems necessary.

LIVE AND LET LIVE:

The point here is that couples have a clear understanding that they cannot live together as husband and wife. They wish to maintain their relationship as devoted friends. In that situation, they will not let the families interfere in the issue and shall decide on their own. They handle the situation in a subtle manner, and they come to an advocate only to execute it in the court of law.

The other situation where they will come to a decision after pending cases is either for divorce on various grounds, restitution of conjugal rights, domestic violence, or maintenance.

I have handled all these types of cases in my 25 years of practice. The intriguing aspect is that these cases often take years to resolve. My style of approaching these cases is very different. I always approach cases from a different perspective, focusing on saving the client's mental distress, time, and money. Below is a list of the interesting cases I have handled and provided quick remedies to my clients.

NO MESSING AND NOT READY TO CLEAN THE DIRTY LINEN IN PUBLIC

1. An intriguing case I handled a year ago for an NRI couple. They separated because they couldn't live together as husband and wife, but they could be friends. They traveled all the way from Poland.

They reached me through their family friend, who believed that I would get justice for them at the earliest. When my client first met me, he said, Madam, I lost my life, but at least I wish to save my job. Since he was from Pune and his wife was in Chennai, the surprising element was that he was staying at her house and was taken care of with good hospitality. There were only three weeks left for him to join his job. If delayed, he will lose his job. For all these cases, the statutory period is 6 months.

Since I was updated with day today's amendments, exactly in

8 days, I finished the entire court process and got the judgment on the 15th day. On the 9th day, he flew back to Poland, promptly reporting to his workplace and retaining his job. He called me from Poland and appreciated my swift work, which has not only helped to retain his job but also resulted in a slight increment for his earlier project, which he never expected. This is how I help my clients according to their needs but not for their wants.

2. Another mutual consent couple had no common person to communicate with. The wife, a busy employed woman, was exhausted and had recently recovered from her mental trauma. Then, I acted as a common person between the couple during the COVID-19 pandemic, a time when travel to cities was banned. In this case, my client had only a job, while her husband was unemployed. She managed his entire journey from Sikkim to Chennai, his stay in Chennai, and all court expenses, including advocate fees. She asked me how fast I could give her relief.

I said that since it was Covid time, I could not commit to the time frame but that I would do my best to get her the results fast. We know miracles happen. Her struggle fell on the ears of the universe, and the whole court process was completed within 19 days. She also got her verdict on the same day since it was Family court. The judge demonstrated compassion by understanding the practical difficulties and providing legal assistance throughout the entire process, without going above and beyond.

On the day of departure, he said to my client that he would be her best friend and literally felt very sorry for missing her in his life. He said this could be a better gift to her for her patience during the 6 years of married life where he was very harsh to her.

It was akin to a mutual confession, as both of them departed with no regrets or feelings of guilt.

After all, we are all mankind, and love and compassion are there in each and every human being. Some demonstrate, and others don't know how to demonstrate. I understood very clearly that people's skills are very important for overcoming any tough situation. Every case was a positive experience for me in my professional career.

DIVORCE IS VERY COSTLY:

1. I would like to mention another pathetic case that was also finished during the Covid period. There was a previous case between them. And he was also an NRI. It was pending for nearly two years. Then COVID came. The case continued without any progress in the courts. I utilized the free time in doing regular talks with the other side's advocate and slowly made up his mind for settlement.

In the meantime, due to this trauma, my client was taking assistance for severe stress levels where he could not control his mental agony. This was told to me by his father in Chennai and his mother literally wept and was very scared about her son's condition. The other side's counsel was demanding one crore of rupees as alimony on behalf of his client. My clients were ready only for half of it.

Upon appearing before the courts, both fathers were represented as power of attorney. Both the counsel stated that they are currently engaged in settlement negotiations. Suddenly the judge asked in the open court, "Was it your expectation for settlement?" Unexpectedly facing this question in public, the girl's father unexpectedly responded with a settlement of 50 lakhs. It was a tremendous help for us and my client. Then we withdrew this case and filed a petition for divorce by mutual consent and settled the case finally by paying 46 lakhs as alimony.

They both appeared online during the COVID period and eventually separated. Then, after 6 months, my client informed me that he had married a girl who appreciated his shortcomings and accepted him for all he is. There is always an afterlife with bright hopes.

2. Another case was also finished during COVID. Here my client filed a case for divorce. He was also an NRI client. In this case, it was a love-cum- arranged marriage. My client converted himself to the religion of his spouse. My client was placed in a reputable company, having a decent income, a soft-spoken man, highly knowledgeable, and totally a reasonable person. In our society, above all this, there are people who are very keen about caste.

My client was always humiliated by the parents of his spouse because of their caste discrimination. They never accepted the marriage at heart. The couple were happily living in Chennai by buying a flat and leading a peaceful life with their kid. The evil mind of the other party's parents stated their foul play and slowly poisoned the mind of his wife and drew out my client from his own house. Once they drove him out of his house, he filed for divorce.

The other side did not have any allegations, but she was a puppet in the hands of her parents. Then, after mediation through both the counsels, my client settled for the welfare of their son and his wife. He not only gave the flat owned by him, also paid 20 lakhs in cash. Finally, I helped my client by filing a mutual application and got him a divorce.

In this case I really felt pathetic for the girl. I believe that she truly yearned for a genuine man in her life. Every year during the New Year, he used to wish me. When I asked him if he would marry again, he replied that he would not be able to come out of that relationship mentally, so he wishes to be single. Many times, fate works differently. The sad part is that due to caste differences, this marriage failed, not because of the difference of opinion between the parties to it.

So, readers, beware that you don't involve your parents in your own family life, as you may lose your valuable matrimonial life because of it. Life is a bigger picture; it should not be shattered due to flimsy reasons.

After struggling to make a decision:

Another client of mine who is a teacher carried her legal battle for nearly 14 years on various litigations initiated by her, like maintenance and restitution of conjugal rights, while the divorce case was initiated by her husband. She was extremely determined to provide her son with a father figure. Despite the absence of fatherly love and affection, his longing for his father persisted.

So, this poor lady didn't give up her hopes and was carrying the battle for 14 long years. The son one day came to the court when he was in 10th grade to see his father. All his hopes were dashed when he saw his father in person, as he never bothered to inquire about him. Then he decided that he doesn't need his father anymore.

My client then took a drastic step to disown her husband and decided to get a divorce by mutual consent by getting an alimony of 10 lakhs. This long wait moved her to make a decision that this dead marriage will never work. Now she is raising her son as a single parent and successfully graduated him as an engineer, emphasizing all the values of a decent human being. Courage is the key to survival.

MUTUAL CONSENT SOMETIMES PLEASURE AND SOMETIMES PAIN:

Another heartbreaking case during the initial days of my practice way back in the year 2002, when a very limited number of divorce cases were filed in courts. The case number was a single digit. This divorce happened due to the arrogant egos of two families where the couples were the prey.

Although neither of them intended to leave, their respective family members forced them to do so. Their final hearing fell on a Friday. On that day, they both had to exchange their belongings. They forcibly reclaimed the Thali (mangal sutra) from the girl, an incident that remains vividly etched in my memory. The true fact is that the thali need not be returned to the husband. It is a gift given to the wife. It is her property. They arrogantly got back the thali. She cried very hard in the court premises itself. There was no other way, as both of them agreed to return all the articles belonging to each other.

This scenario has struck me very much. Even though as advocates we advised our client's family not to go for a divorce, the ego and arrogance of the client's family finally succeeded. Even we advocates have our own boundaries and limits to restrict our interference. We can advise, but the ultimate decision is in the hands of the clients, especially in matrimonial disputes.

In this case, the parents' ego truly took a toll. They lost their valuable lives for someone's ego. Sometimes, couples entrust their life decisions to the wrong hands, leading to lifelong pain. Although this incident occurred in 2002, it continues to recur in the lives of many couples today. There is always pain and suffering.

AUTHOR'S EXPERIENCE:

Dear readers, even if you think you need a divorce, explore all the options to stay together. We all belong to mankind; every one of us has feelings. Outsiders and passersby are merely observers. They will throw out their own suggestions.

Dear readers, always allow your inner voice to answer your doubts. You can only hear it when your mind is calm. First, calm down all your emotions and allow your inner voice to answer all your doubts. That voice will be very soft and genuine. The answer will not be what you expect. Only the truth will be revealed to you. Everyone knows TRUTH is always challenging to digest. Always truth alone triumphs. Accept the hard truth and carry on with your journey with no regrets, blame, guilt, or pain. Only the person in trouble can figure out the exact situation and remedy.

Life has problems, but relationship issues affect the individual and the close-knit family. Day by day, the issue will gradually become more pressing. If a case is pending in court and dragging on till the disposal of the entire case, the family and friends will be disturbed and will also be undergoing severe mental agony.

Wise people always choose the option of getting a divorce by mutual consent. The time to endure the agony is short, and the relationship will end without regrets, guilt, or mutual accusations, at least in some cases. Live and let live is the best attitude to move forward in life. In some situations, the marriage will not work.

At that point in time, first approach an advocate to learn the legal consequences of matrimonial decisions and the time and money involved. Then, make sure to consult with marriage counselors who can assist you and provide guidance on how to avoid the current mess in your life.

After this, embark on a 21-day challenge within yourself to learn how to quiet the chatterbox noise in your mind. When you can hear the soft voice giving you high hopes, there is still a chance for living.

But even after following all these, if the noise is still uncontrollable, then you need to repeat the exercise twice or thrice. Then finally you will start realizing that if you stop putting the wood to burn, the burning stops. You will gradually come to understand that altering your identity will bring about a transformation in all aspects of your life.

This mindset will help you resolve your marital issue and bring clarity to your work, health, finances, and life. Then you will start feeling that you are living in heaven. There will be a paradigm shift in your thoughts.

Life is a human game. So do not keep your priority on material things, which are perishable. If the relationship between the couples is strong, they can win over this world. E.g., Mr. Murthy and Mrs. Sudha Murthy of Infosys. I can provide you with a list of numerous couples who began their journey together and have achieved significant success.

My suggestion would be to try all the possible methods, as stated above, to make the marital tie exist. If you can't continue, make the big decision to leave without hurting, bothering, or guilting yourself. Then go ahead with your decision to **LIVE AND LET LIVE.**

DEVELOPMENTS OF LAW IN GIVING SPEEDY REMEDIES.

We have seen that the waiting period is six months, and it can be extended until eighteen months to reach the finality of a case filed on the grounds of mutual consent.

You all know that **INDIA** is a **DEMOCRATIC** country. It is **OF THE PEOPLE, BY THE PEOPLE, AND FOR THE PEOPLE.**

The legislation clearly states that it must protect all citizens without resorting to traditional methods or maintaining a chaotic system. Since we live in a modernized world, the legislation is updated to meet the needs of the current society.

The statutory time for a mutual consent case is 6 months. The legislation felt that those who are litigating for a long time have certain parameters to get out of the mental agony even before 6 months. You would have read it in the above cases I have handled.

The ***famous case [11]Amardeep Singh vs. Harveen Kaur, was heard by the Hon'ble Supreme Court on September 12th, 2017. The mode of citation is 2017 (8) SCC 746.*** It has given the following guidelines.

"Applying the above to the present situation, we are of the view that where the court dealing with a matter is satisfied that a case is made out to waive the statutory period under Section 13-B (2), it can do so after considering the following:

i) The statutory period of six months specified in Section 13-B (2), in addition to the statutory period of one year under Section 13-B (1), for separation of parties is already over before the first motion itself;

ii) All efforts for mediation/conciliation, including efforts in terms of Order XXIII Rule 3 CPC/Section 23(2) of the Act/ Section 9 of the Family Courts Act to reunite the parties, have failed, and there is no likelihood of success in that direction by any further efforts;

[11] - Sourced from indiakanoon.org

iii) The parties have genuinely settled their differences, including alimony, custody of the child, or any other pending issues between them.

iv) The waiting period will only prolong their agony.

One week after the first motion, you can file the waiver application, providing the justification for the waiver request.

If the above conditions are satisfied, the waiver of the waiting period for the second motion will be at the discretion of the concerned court."

We should always believe the system is working for that. We know traffic signals are there to prevent accidents. In some situations, the traffic signals may take the life of a person in the ambulance. So, can we now say, "Remove all the traffic signals?" The situation will worsen to the point where even a healthy man crossing a road could potentially lose his life.

In the judgment, it is stated that it is the discretion of the court; it is not the same procedure that is necessarily to be followed by every judge. So first, when you have to approach a court for a case, you need to understand the nuances of the court and the advocate you are choosing. Go to a specialist advocate who has already dealt with these types of cases at large. They keep themselves updated on the latest amendments to the cases, ensuring prompt remedies for clients experiencing mental agony. Gujarat High Court Judgment in a Mutual Consent Divorce Appeal Not Maintainable against Decree. Hindu Marriage Act S.13-B & 19(2) & 28. In a case of divorce by mutual consent, the issue of appealability of the decree was raised. Both parties, represented by their respective advocates, voluntarily consented to the divorce. They jointly moved an application seeking waiver of the statutory cooling-off period. The Court, upon satisfaction that the consent was free from coercion, undue influence, or fraud, granted the waiver. The Court recorded that the marital relationship had irretrievably broken down and was beyond reconciliation. The decree of divorce was passed with the express and informed consent of both spouses. As per settled legal principles, no appeal lies against a decree passed with the consent of the parties. The contention that the consent was vitiated was found to be base-less. The Court affirmed that once parties consciously choose to dis-solve their marriage, they cannot challenge the decree. Accordingly, the appeal was held to be not maintainable.

CHAPTER 3

I - INITIATING FOR MAINTENANCE

EITHER OF THE SPOUSES CAN CLAIM MAINTENANCE:

The law is equal to all citizens of India. The general public will reject the myth that only wives and children receive maintenance. The legislators established this ideology even in 1955, when only 1% of the women's population held employment. This particular section may come as a surprise to many. The legislation understood the power of a woman way back in the year 1955. Great leaders like Jansi Rani, Mother Teresa, Karaikal Ammaiyar, Indira Gandhi, etc., to demonstrate that women are not the weaker sex. They are the shakti and force behind anyone. It may be for a man, for the family, or for society.

We know very well that the whole world is a male-dominated society. We should also appreciate that if injustice is happening to a woman, the men will be the first to raise their voices and protect her from all the disasters. E.g., Rajaram Mohan Roy abolished Sati, Pudhumai Bharathi, and Thanthai Periyar, who broke the myth in the minds of the people about women. She is a living being; she has the right to live, do wonders in life, and also be a part of building society.

They eliminated the societal stereotypes that women are only suited for childrearing, raising children, cooking, and other household tasks. These gentlemen proved that the home department is the powerful agency in the legislation and exhibited that women are on par with men in all aspects and all fields of work.

The framework of the legislation is awesome. The interpreters and the people who want to use law as a shield and a sword misuse the entire purpose. Therefore, understanding the clear meaning of the framework is crucial, and we should strive to strengthen it further. We experience this judgment, reap its full benefits, and ensure the protection of every citizen within the framework of legislation.

Dear readers, understand our Indian culture well and try to demonstrate that you have come up from this rich culture. Ancient history says all Indians were rich, self-sufficient, and helped each other with their resources. There was no poverty in the minds and attitudes of the people. Only due to the invasion of British and other foreign invaders did we Indians lose all our resources.

Rebuilding was not a problem because many followed the culture and lived as examples, like Ratan Tata, Palam Kalyanasundaram, etc. And we Indians have proved to the whole world that **LIVING IS FOR GIVING.** When Swami Vivekananda went to the USA to give speeches, he stated that charity is the only way to become rich. Many people in the USA and other foreign countries appreciated these teachings, emphasizing the importance of giving charity and leading a fulfilling life. A rich mindset will always be in giving mode. The poor mindset will always be in the fear of losing. If you live in

Indian culture for one day, you'll be hooked for life. It is there in our DNA.

The negative mindset prevalent in our society today is a cultural catastrophe. If we believe that we share the genes of our great ancestors, we can always rebuild this mindset. We all know that if one man can do it, another following the same principles can. We know copying is easy. In today's fast world, everyone is ready to copy how to grow rich in one year, one month, one week, one day, one hour, one minute, or even the next moment. They believe that money can solve all their problems.

The difficult truth is that money alone cannot solve all the problems without rebuilding the richest culture of our society. We Indians are the pioneers to demonstrate the RICHEST CULTURE of how a society has to be. The society is always functioning in the methodology of TRADITION PLUS INNOVATION. So, there is always a possible way to rebuild and recreate our forgotten culture.

These are the reasons why the legislation felt both men and women are equals and also gave the opportunity for men to also understand that he is also a human being and also needs support when he has fallen down. At that point in time, if the woman is employed and if she has the earning capacity, she should maintain her husband for food, clothing, and shelter. In today's world, a significant number of women are employed, and the percentage of women who complete their education surpasses that of men. Even otherwise, women want to empower themselves like men. Employment not only adds credits to men, but also women wish to add credits for her talents.

INTERIM MAINTENANCE FOR THE SPOUSE NOT ABLE TO MAINTAIN THEMSELVES.

Section 24 of the Hindu Marriage Act reads as follows:

It is possible for the court to order the respondent to pay the petitioner the costs of the proceeding and an amount each month during the proceeding that the court thinks is reasonable based on the petitioner's income and the respondent's income. This can happen if it appears to the court that either the wife or the husband does not have enough independent income to support herself or himself and pay for the necessary costs of the proceeding. This can be asked for by either the wife or the husband.

[Provided that the application for the payment of the expenses of the proceeding and such monthly sum during the proceeding shall, as far as possible, be disposed of within sixty days from the date of service of notice on the wife or the husband, as the case may be.].

AUTHOR'S EXPLANATION:

If you claim maintenance, as per this section, either of the spouses can claim maintenance. This is an interim relief. You can benefit from the claimed relief as long as the case is pending. Once the case attains its finality, if maintenance is ordered, it would cease to exist.

As per this section, either the husband or wife who has

1. Lack of sufficient independent income,
2. For the husband or wife's support with monthly maintenance

and the necessary expenses of the proceeding,

3. On request by the wife or husband, the court may order the respondent to pay the petitioner's proceeding expenses and monthly maintenance.
4. That sum, having regard to the petitioner's own income and the income of the respondent, may seem to the court to be reasonable.
5. Provided that the application for the payment of the expenses of thc proceeding,
6. As part of the ongoing maintenance,
7. Shall be disposed of within sixty days from the date of service of notice on the wife or the husband, as the case may be.

CASE STUDY:

VERDICT GIVEN BY DELHI HIGH COURT

[12]***Chetram vs. Karishma of November 21, 2023, Mat. Appeal (F.C.) No. 196/2023 was filed under the Hindu Marriage Act, 1955, Section 24.*** The wife was given maintenance pendente lite of Rs. 30,000/- p.m., but the husband appealed because the wife was already getting Rs. 21,000/- p.m. under the D.V. Act and had a reasonable educational background as a graduate from Delhi University. The court held that refusing to work without a good reason or sincere job-seeking efforts should not put financial responsibility on the other person.

[12] - Sourced from indiakanoon.org

Section 24 is gender neutral—maintenance pendente lite and litigation expenses should be awarded with the objective of providing relief to the spouse who is unable to maintain and support themselves during the pendency of proceedings. Mathematical precision is not required. Therefore, we modify the impugned order and dispose of the appeal in the aforementioned terms.

PERMANENT ALIMONY AFTER THE FINALITY OF THE CASE.

This section clearly states that the award of maintenance is pending in the case. Section 25 of the act clearly states the permanent maintenance awarded.

Section 25 of the Hindu Marriage Act reads as follows:

Permanent alimony and maintenance

(1) Any court exercising jurisdiction under this Act may, at the time of passing any decree or at any time subsequent thereto, on application made to it for the purpose by either the wife or the husband, as the case may be, order that the respondent shall pay to the applicant for her or his maintenance and support such gross sum or such monthly or periodical sum for a term not exceeding the life of the applicant as, having regard to the respondent's own income and other property, if any, the income and other property of the applicant 1 [the conduct of the parties and other circumstances of the case], it may seem to the court to be just, and any such payment may be secured, if necessary, by a charge on the immovable property

of the respondent.

(2) If the court is satisfied that there is a change in the circumstances of either party at any time after it has made an order under sub-section (1), it may, at the instance of either party, vary, modify, or rescind any such order in such manner as the court may deem just.

(3) If the court is satisfied that the party in whose favour an order has been made under this section has remarried or, if such party is the wife, that she has not remained chaste, or, if such party is the husband, that he has had sexual intercourse with any woman outside wedlock, [it may at the instance of the other party vary, modify or rescind any such order in such manner as the court may deem just].

AUTHOR'S EXPLANATION:

You can access this section at the conclusion of the case or even after it has concluded. Either the wife or the husband, depending on the situation, must make an application before the court. If the court thinks fit, it shall pass orders in favour of the petitioner, and the respondent shall pay to her or him maintenance in such a gross sum.

The applicant may order the maintenance on a monthly basis or as a periodic sum for a term not exceeding their lifetime. If the ordered maintenance is not paid by the respondent, it could be recovered by creating a charge over the immovable property, and in the case of a government servant, the salary could be attached to the maintenance amount.

The legislature's forward-thinking approach has resulted in no major amendments to this act to date. They have framed the act in such a manner that it has to suit all types of situations people may face. They state that if the court believes either party's circumstances have changed after it has passed orders, it may modify or revoke any such order at either party's request.

If the court is satisfied that the party in whose favour an order has been made under this section falls under these criteria of the change of circumstances, the court may vary, modify or rescind its orders and shall render justice to the party affected. As per the fundamental rights, there is always "**EQUALITY BEFORE LAW.**" This section itself demonstrates the same.

1. If the party in whose favour maintenance is ordered has remarried,
2. If such party is the wife and she has not remained chaste,
3. If the husband is the party in question, and he has engaged in sexual relations with any woman outside of marriage.
4. Both men and women are equal under the law. And regarding the maintenance, there is equal opportunity for both. Therefore, if both parties submit an application with valid reasons and fulfilled conditions, the deserving person will receive permanent alimony.

As per the new development of Legislation the spouse who ever claims maintenance or permanent alimony should submit the assets and liabilities statements of each other to determine the awarding of maintenance. If any false claim is proved by the other side it amounts to Perjury a criminal offence. Dear readers, be aware of the current situation and give all true statements to avoid punishments of imprisonment.

Case conducted by me

In a unique case, the court granted the husband's divorce application and granted the wife permanent alimony. The facts of this case are that the husband was very prompt in paying the monthly maintenance to the wife, even though he was finding it difficult to gct along with thc family relationship, as she was suffering from a partial mental disorder and was also not cooperating for the treatment. Hence the husband filed a petition for divorce on the grounds of cruelty and desertion.

The court understood the real situation and granted alimony to her as a legal right, in spite of her partial mental disorder. Both parties received fair relief in the order. And moreover, the husband was also very compassionate toward her and paid the maintenance awarded by the court. In this case, the child's custody lies with the father.

This case is equitable and benefits both parties. Courts consistently show that the legal system will provide justice to litigating parties. In matrimonial disputes, court is the proper forum to grant orders for restitution or separation. This is interlinked with the properties of the parties. Only the decree of a court of law will put an end to all other benefits for the parties.

Case Study:

M.P. High Court Judgement Laws (MPH)-2025-3-8

Permanent Alimony - Necessity of Formal Application

Hindu Marriage Act Section.28(4), 25, 13(1) & 13(1) (i-a) - The High Court reaffirmed that a spouse cannot be directed to pay permanent alimony without filing a formal application under Section.25 of the Act. Section.25 provides that a court may grant permanent alimony and maintenance only upon an application made by either spouse. The court must consider the financial standing of both parties, their conduct, and other relevant circumstances before passing such an order. It was emphasised that at least an express request for alimony is necessary, whether in a written statement or through a separate application. The husband had appealed against the trial court's order under Section. 25, which directed him to pay Rs. 12,000 per month to his wife as maintenance. Despite the wife's lack of request, the trial court approved the divorce decision based on cruelty and awarded alimony. The High Court observed that the trial court erred in granting maintenance suo-motu without any formal plea. Relying on judicial precedents, the High Court concluded that the trial court lacked jurisdiction to award alimony in such circumstances. Consequently, the High Court set aside the trial court's order granting maintenance under Section. 25.

ASKING FOR SRIDHANA ARTICLES:

Under section 27 of the Hindu Marriage Act, the wife can claim the Sridhana articles. It is the asset given by the wife's parents during her marriage for her welfare. Therefore, the court is responsible for ensuring the proper return of the articles to the wife upon request. The husband can also file a petition to return the Sridhana articles to the wife through court to avoid unnecessary litigation.

Section 27 of the Hindu Marriage Act reads as follows:

27. Disposal of property—In any proceeding under this Act, the court may make such provisions in the decree as it deems just and proper with respect to any property presented at or about the time of marriage that may belong jointly to both the husband and the wife.

AUTHOR'S EXPLANATION:

For the return of Sridhana property, the court may pass orders based on the evidence placed by the petitioner to prove their case. Thus, if the court deems it just and proper to award the bride any property presented at or near the time of marriage, which may belong jointly or severally to the husband or wife.

In Hindu culture, the bride typically receives the Sridhana property during the marriage ceremony for security purposes. In Hindu marriages, both movable and immovable properties are given to the bride for her future well-being.

Case study:

Return of Gold Ornaments—Entitlement

The wife argued that she received 6 ½ sovereigns of gold as part of her marriage. The husband claimed that he had no knowledge about the quantity of gold brought with her or that she was wearing all gold. When she was taken for delivery by parental house testimony corroborated by a certified copy of an extract of the marriage register, the wife was entitled to the return of gold ornaments.[13] AIR 2020 Kerala 188(B).

The individual making the assertion must provide proof. The onus of proof rests with the individual asserting its existence. Dear readers, when it comes to property, we have to be cautious. In matrimonial disputes, families allocate Sridhana property for the bride's welfare, taking into account their respective statuses. Couples today take these disputes seriously due to the rise in greed and insecurity.

[13] - Sourced from indiakanoon.org

CHAPTER 4

V- VISITATION RIGHTS OF THE MINOR CHILDREN

INTERIM CUSTODY, MAINTENANCE, AND EDUCATIONAL EXPENSES FOR THE MINOR CHILDREN:

Section 26 of the Hindu Marriage Act reads as follows:

Custody of children.—In any proceeding under this Act, the court may, from time to time, pass such interim orders and make such provisions in the decree as it may deem just and proper with respect to the custody, maintenance and education of minor children, consistently with their wishes, wherever possible, and may, after the decree, upon application by petition for the purpose, make from time to time, all such orders and provisions with respect to the custody, maintenance and education of such children as might have been made by such decree or interim orders in case the proceeding for obtaining such decree were still pending, and the court may also from time to time revoke, suspend or vary any such orders and provisions previously made:

[Provided that the application with respect to the maintenance and education of the minor children, pending the proceeding for obtaining such decree, shall, as far as possible, be disposed of within sixty days from the date of service of notice on the respondent.]

AUTHOR'S EXPLANATION:

Regarding child custody, this act can grant only interim custody. For permanent custody, you have to approach the Guardian Wards Act. The court in any proceeding under this Act, from time to time, passes such interim orders. The court will grant these orders to facilitate the love, care, and affection of both the child and the respondent. If the court feels just and proper with respect to the custody, maintenance, and education of minor children and consistent with their wishes, it shall pass orders in favour of the applicant.

Due to a change in circumstances regarding the custody, maintenance, and education of these children, the court has the authority to revoke, suspend, or vary any previous orders and provisions, even after interim orders have been passed. If the maintenance and educational expenses of the minor children are pending, the proceeding shall be disposed of within sixty days from the date of service of notice on the respondent.

The law not only protects the rights of the husband or the wife. It also protects the welfare of minor children. It clearly understands the minds of the children and sees whether the other parent is really interested in the welfare of the minor child. There are certain parameters to understand whether the parent claiming interim custody of the minor child has created assets by paying any insurance or any future investments or any small savings for the welfare of the minor child, paying school fees, or tuition fees. Moreover, the court will appreciate primarily the willingness of the minor child.

Both the parents can fight for the custody of the minor child only till the age of 18 years. After that it is the absolute right of the child to decide whether to be the father or the mother. Only the husband and wife can file for divorce. It will not extend to the child. The biological father or the mother will not change at any point in time the property rights of the child.

During the divorce between the husband and the wife, they can restrict their bonding. They are not allowed to include any clauses regarding the future benefits of the child, nor can they restrict the child's birth right to the property of both parents. It is up to the child to decide after attaining majority whether he or she needs to claim it or forgo it.

The law understands clearly that the children are the future of our nation. It gives 100% protection and care for the welfare of the minor children. The court can demand all maintenance, custody, and educational expenses while the case is pending. Once the case is over, if the spouse taking care of the children wants to claim permanent custody, he or she needs to file a Guardian Wards Original Petition. This is the process through which they can obtain relief for their minor children.

CASE STUDY:

The Supreme Court of India rendered a verdict.

Parents **who are denied custody shall have** the right to talk to their child every day.

[14] ***Yashita Sahu v/s State of Rajasthan on 20 January 2020— Crl. App. No. 127 of 2020***— Custody of a minor child— The

[14] - Sourced from indiakanoon.org

concept of 'contact rights' is also important for the development of a child, especially in cases where both parents live in different states or countries. Unless there are special circumstances to take a different view, the parent who is denied custody of the child should have the right to talk to his/her child for 5–10 minutes every day. This will help in maintaining and improving the bond between the child and the parent who is denied custody. If we can't give the child one happy home with two parents, let them have two happy homes with one parent each. (Para 22)

CHAPTER 5

O- OFFERING JUDICIAL SEPARATION

WHAT IS JUDICIAL SEPARATION?

SECTION 10 OF THE HINDU MARRIAGE ACT READS AS FOLLOWS:

Judicial separation. 1 (1) Either party to a marriage, whether solemnized before or after the commencement of this Act, may present a petition praying for a decree for judicial separation on any of the grounds specified in sub-section (1) of section 13, and in the case of a wife also on any of the grounds specified in sub-section (2) thereof, as grounds on which a petition for divorce might have been presented.

(2) Where a decree for judicial separation has been passed, it shall no longer be obligatory for the petitioner to cohabit with the respondent, but the court may, on the application by petition of either party and on being satisfied of the truth of the statements made in such petition, rescind the decree if it considers it just and reasonable to do so.

SECTION 13(1A) (i) OF THE HINDU MARRIAGE ACT READS AS FOLLOWS:

Section 13 (1A): Either party to a marriage, whether solemnized before or after the commencement of this Act, may also present a petition for the dissolution of the marriage by a

decree of divorce on the ground.

(i)that there has been no resumption of cohabitation as between the parties to the marriage for a period of [one year] or upwards after the passing of a decree for judicial separation in a proceeding to which they were parties.

AUTHOR'S EXPLANATION:

In Hindu law, judicial separation means the same term as in other personal laws, such as the Christian Divorce Act and the Special Marriage Act. This legal option allows married individuals subject to personal laws to live apart without terminating their marriage. In contrast to divorce, which ends the marriage, legal separation lets the couple live apart while still being married. The importance of this law idea lies in the fact that it gives married couples another option. No one will refer to them as divorcees. But how long will they be able to enjoy the decree's benefits?

According to the law, if one party to a marriage does not return to the matrimonial home after a period of one year or more following the issuance of a judicial separation decree in a case, this can serve as grounds for divorce.

Therefore, the court provides a period of time for them to resolve their misunderstandings, allowing them to live apart, understand their differences, and acknowledge their continued status as husband and wife. And they can resume without any hard feelings. Time is the best healer of all injuries.

The main purpose of this section is to promote family harmony and to provide an opportunity for the couples to escape from divorce. Generally, the difference of opinion creeps up when the couple is between 45 and 50 years old. By the time their children had grown up, they would have reached the age of marriage. At that point, both the husband and wife will make such decisions to uphold the family's reputation and prioritize the welfare of their children. They want to avoid embarrassing themselves in public and becoming a source of gossip, as this could lead to difficulties in their children's family life.

Life offers separate question papers to each individual. Some questions are easy to ask, some are hard to answer, and some are very sensitive and personal. Others can comment, criticize, and offer suggestions, but only the person going through the rough phase can express their issue. The audience should respect their choices rather than make up nonsense.

The legislature, in its rich experience, has created a section like this to help the couples, whatever their ages may be, to live a joyful life for the betterment of society. The implementation of these sorts of acts is to tell society that both men and women are equal, and the state has the right and responsibility to protect each and every citizen of the country.

WHO CAN ASK FOR A JUDICIAL SEPARATION?

Either the husband or the wife may seek the court to separate them. You can ask for the separation by submitting a petition to the appropriate court. These are the reasons why a judge can separate a husband and wife: in the case of a wife, any of the reasons in sub-section (2) can also be used.

The court decision for separation means that the couple is no longer required to live together and can choose to live apart.

WHAT DO YOU DO TO GET RELIEF IN COURT?

The Family Court of the original civil jurisdiction must hear every case under the Hindu Marriage Act. You can file the petition in any of the subcourts if there is no Family Court available.

1. The marriage took place.
2. The respondent resides there.
3. The last married couple cohabitated.
4. The petitioner is a woman who currently resides in her home.

GROUNDS:

The reasons for judicial separation are the same as the reasons for divorce. In short, we can explore here and shall explain in the 6th chapter. The grounds are:

These grounds include adultery, cruelty, desertion, unsound mind, venereal disease, renunciation of the world, conversion to any other religion, and not being heard for more than 7 years.

Additional Grounds That Can Be Claimed Only by the Wife:

These grounds include bigamy, rape, sodomy, or bestiality; the non-resumption of cohabitation following a decree or order of maintenance; and the repudiation of marriage.

CASE LAWS:

1. [15]***Subbarama Reddiar v. Sakaswathi Ammal (1966):*** The Madras High Court discussed at length what judicial separation (on grounds of adultery) is and how it works. It also stated that it can only happen for the grounds stated in Section 13 of the Hindu Marriage Act, 1955.

If a spouse files for judicial separation and can show that their partner is living in adultery, the petition may be granted.

2. [16]***Rohini Kumari v. Narendra Singh (1971):*** The case: If one partner (in this case, the husband) leaves their partner, the other person can file for legal separation if she does not want to live with the husband. It was also decided that if a couple gets a court order for a legal separation, the wife can ask her husband for support under both the Hindu Marriage Act and the Hindu Adoption and Maintenance Act.

[15] - Sourced from indiakanoon.org
[16] - Sourced from indiakanoon.org

Some ways in which judicial separation and divorce are different:

JUDICIAL SEPARATION	DIVORCE
Section 10 of the Hindu Marriage Act 1955 says that a request for Judicial separation can be made at any time after marriage.	Section 13 of the Hindu Marriage Act 1955 says that you can't file for divorce until you've been married for at least one year.
Under the Hindu Marriage Act, judicial separation means that the marriage is put on hold for a short time.	When a couple gets divorced, they are no longer married.
Once a decree of Judicial Separation is in passed, neither party cannot get married again.	Once the divorce is finalized and the appeal period ends or is over the couple can get married again.
Any party can ask the court to cancel the decree of judicial separation, as long as the court is satisfied.	A divorce decree can't be rescinded, but it can be appealed.

WHY TO OPT FOR JUDICIAL SEPARATION IN CERTAIN CASES:

When couples feel that the difference of opinion is less, then they can opt for judicial separation. It is a temporary suspension of marriage, and marriage is a bigger entity where small issues should not defeat the larger benefit. The couple cannot remarry after passing a decree of judicial separation. Resolving differences of opinion increases the chances of reunion. To keep the marital tie alive, it is always better to opt for judicial separation.

First, couples with children should try this remedy, then consider divorce. These days, the number of single parents is increasing. Even school application forms contain this column that needs to be filled. It is a really pathetic situation for the kids. The value of relationships is very much shrunken. In fact, the sibling ratio has gradually come down due to money inflation, the cost of living, and various other factors. These are the reasons we should opt for judicial separation rather than divorce.

PHYSIOLOGICAL FACTOR

Any dispute between couples is always a nightmare, and they could not lead a normal life. That fear of losing will always be constant in one party who wishes to save the marriage. It is a challenging fact to understand that "life is too short" to mess up with the partner for flimsy reasons. Many couples struggle to manage their stress levels and find it difficult to focus on their work and other daily responsibilities. This not only affects the couples, but in case they have kids, it mainly affects the kids. Then it affects the parents and the immediate circle of relatives. Until the dispute reaches its finality, the mental agony and pain will be a compliment for all in the family.

CASE HANDLED BY ME:

A few years ago, for one of my clients, I filed a case for judicial separation for a client who was then aged 40 years and was well employed. My client had such faith in her husband that she entrusted him with all her ATM cards, not even bothering to store the secret PIN numbers. The husband handled all the financial responsibilities. In spite of my client being so open and truthful, her husband was a hardened drunk and used to abuse her verbally, physically, mentally, and monetarily. Since she was a God-fearing Christian and had a grown-up boy and girl child, my client said she would not divorce him and would wait and see whether he transformed himself and joined the matrimonial home.

But to her shock and surprise, she got the information that he was having a concubine. Her unconditional belief in him never allowed her to think that his illicit relationship would be true. Then one day the other woman herself called my client and informed her about the illicit relationship. Later, when my client enquired about this to her husband, he confessed the same. My client was totally shattered into pieces, and when checking all her bank accounts and savings, she was left with only 6000 in her account. She realized that all the money, savings, fixed deposits, and insurance were all closed, and she wiped off her husband. All her 12 years of married life and her finances vanished in a moment. She found herself and her children abandoned in the matrimonial house.

The only hope she had was her job and her aged parents. His siblings don't show much interest in him. Everyone has their own commitments. She never gave up. She fought the case, and I assisted her in securing the necessary funds for the children's education. His son reached the age of majority while the case was still ongoing. Her husband stopped the aid given to the son. She never gave up. She raised the children single-handedly. Poor women were not able to answer the peer pressure from society, family, and friends. She was constantly mentally disturbed and faced financial hardships. Her aged parents consistently provided a glimmer of hope, despite their struggles to manage their affairs.

My client finally decided that there is no point in living with him again, and after a few years, she decided to get a divorce from him on the insistence of the children. She made this decision after managing the case for a few years. It took nearly 4 years for her to take this bold decision, too, for the welfare of the kids. Then finally I helped her to get a house in favour of the children, and she never took even a single penny from him towards her maintenance. The house she acquired for her children was entirely funded by the earnings and savings she received from him for their upbringing.

After seven years, the case underwent a conversion to mutual consent and received relief. Some cases persist for an extended period. There are genuine cases where they don't decide hastily. It involves trust, emotions, and years of living in a married relationship. Finally, she won her battle and got relieved from the fake relationship without any guilty feelings.

Author's views on this case:

In this particular case, we did not achieve an easy victory. Her husband never used to pay even the maintenance on time. My client understood the practical difficulty of the proceedings, and her patient approach helped her to get the larger relief with ease. It's all about educating the clients. In my experience, I have seen a few clients who were very hasty in getting the things done. I would wish to say that if you wait for your time, surely the advocate can get better results in your case. If there is any hasty decision or nagging attitude from you, then that will be reflected in your case proceedings, resulting in too many losses. Recently I had a chance to see my client. She was very happy, saying that she had begun educating her son abroad for his higher education, and now he is working in the USA as a software engineer. Additionally, she reported that her son had successfully paid off all his educational loans. Her daughter has successfully completed both her college education and her dance training. She expressed her gratitude for my assistance in enhancing her life. Complimenting it, she referred me to a new case for divorce who has been suffering for a long time with mental issues. I am sure that happy clients will always refer back to you. It is my habit to tell myself that I am giving my best when taking up a new case. This gives me lots of clarity and confidence that I will help my clients with their remedies in the appropriate manner. It was a beneficial learning experience for me. I am in the field of lifelong learning. I thank all my clients for giving me the best experience in conducting their cases. Thank you almighty for giving me the opportunity to help the needy who are in trouble.

CHAPTER 6

R—RESTITUTION OF CONJUGAL RIGHTS

SECTION 9 OF THE HINDU MARRIAGE ACT READS AS FOLLOWS:

Restitution of conjugal rights—When either the husband or the wife has, without reasonable excuse, withdrawn from the society of the other, the aggrieved party may apply, by petition, to the district court for restitution of conjugal rights, and the court, on being satisfied of the truth of the statements made in such petition and that there is no legal ground why the application should not be granted, may decree restitution of conjugal rights accordingly.

Explanation—Where a question arises whether there has been reasonable excuse for withdrawal from the society, the burden of proving reasonable excuse shall be on the person who has withdrawn from the society.

AUTHOR'S EXPLANATION:

In simple terms, restitution of conjugal rights means that if either the husband or the wife has broken up with the other person without a good reason, the person who was in a marriage relationship with them can petition the court that has jurisdiction to get their rights back. The court may order restitution of conjugal rights if they are satisfied with the petitioner's true facts and there is no legal reason why the application shouldn't be granted. This means that the respondent spouse, who has left the marriage, must rejoin the petitioner spouse.

Now the question is whether there was a beneficial reason for leaving the marriage. The person who left society will have to prove that there was a beneficial reason.

One of the fundamental reasons people get married is to live together, and each partner has the right to the comfort and company of the other. This is a unique feature; this is what people often call "conjugal rights."

These two things are what the phrase "conjugal rights" means.

1. A couple has the right to spend time with each other.
2. The right to sexual relations with a spouse.
3. WHAT IS RESTITUTION OF CONJUGAL RIGHTS?
    1. The meaning of restitution of conjugal rights means giving back the rights that a married couple had when they were married.
    2. Return of conjugal rights as allowed by Section 9 of the Hindu Marriage Act, 1955.
    3. The objective of Section 9 is to protect the marriage relationship as a holy and legal institution.
    4. Someone who is aggrieved can ask the District Court to restore marital rights if their husband or wife has withdrawn from the other partner's company for unreasonable grounds.

5. The person who has withdrawn away from society has to show that they had a reasonable excuse to do so.
6. The intention of a court's restitution order is to protect the marriage as much as possible by letting the courts step in and help the couple.

What do you need to do to get help under the Restitution of Conjugal Rights Act?

1. Both parties must be formally married to each other.
2. The two parties should stay away from each other's society.
3. This withdrawal has to happen even though there is no valid justification.
4. The assertion that there is no legal reason to reject the order needs to be proven to the court's satisfaction.

What happens when conjugal rights are restored?

1. If the order for restitution of conjugal rights is granted, the respondent will have to move back in with the petitioner.
2. Either party may file for divorce if they don't complete this within a year of the decree's date.

CASE LAWS:

1. In [17]***Saroj Rani v. Sudarshan Kumar Chadha (1984),*** the Supreme Court held that Section 9 of the Hindu Marriage

[17] - Sourced from AIR Law Journal

Act was constitutional because it did not violate any fundamental rights.

In Hinduism, marriage is a sacred event. Hinduism views marriage as the union of two souls. Following Hindu law, getting married comes with certain duties and rights for both people in the marriage.

In the above case, the Supreme Court stated, "The essence of marriage is sharing a common life, sharing all the happiness and all the misery that life has to offer."

When two people get married, they usually plan to live together. One partner may be forced to file a petition if the other fails to comfort them.

2. In [18]***Susila Bai vs. Prem Narayan Rai (AIR 1985),*** the court stated that if a husband left his wife at her father's house and didn't stay in touch with her, that was the same as withdrawing from his wife's social circle, so a decree for restitution could be ordered.

3. In [19]***Tirath Kaur vs. Kirpal Singh (AIR 1996),*** the Punjab and Haryana High Court had to decide if a wife's job could be a "reasonable excuse" to leave her husband's company and stay away from him. The court adopted the usual method and said that the wife's job is not a reasonable excuse for not showing up. The court also said, "The wife's first duty is to respect her husband and stay under his care and protection."

18 - Sourced from AIR Law Journal
19 - Sourced from AIR Law Journal

4. In the case of [20]***Gaya vs. Bhagwati (AIR 1965),*** the Madhya Pradesh High Court said that in Hindu society, the wife has to do what she is supposed to do as a wife in the husband's house and can't make her own decisions.

5. The Allahabad High Court took a progressive decision in the case of [21]***Shanti Devi vs. Ramesh Chandra (AIR 1969).*** After careful consideration, the court decided that if a wife quits her job because it was too hard, that was a reasonable excuse and could be used as evidence in court. So, there could be no decree for restitution.

Under Section 9 of the Hindu Marriage Act, what is a reasonable excuse?

Most of the time, a "reasonable excuse" means:

The reasons why the person can get help with their marital relief.

1. If either partner has done something wrong in the marriage, that isn't a reason for divorce under Section 13 of the Hindu Marriage Act. Still, that misconduct is very bad, so this could also be considered a reasonable excuse.

2. One partner has done or not done something in a relationship that makes living together unacceptable.

[20] - Sourced from AIR Law Journal
[21] - Sourced from AIR Law Journal

Section 9 of the Hindu Marriage Act, 1955, is upheld by the Constitution.

[22]***T. Sareetha vs. T. VenkataSubbaiah (AIR 1983):*** That Section 9 of the Hindu Marriage Act goes against the person's fundamental right to freedom and respect under Article 21 was argued in the Andhra Pradesh High Court. The Andhra Pradesh High Court declared that Section 9 was not allowed by the Constitution because it restricted people's freedom.

The judge said, "If the wife is forced to live with her husband, this will also be against her right to privacy. As well, the court observed that "restitution as a remedy violates the inviolability of the body and mind and invades the marital privacy and domestic intimacies of such a person."

[23]***Saroj Rani vs. Sudarshan Kumar Chandra (AIR 1984 SC):*** The Supreme Court finally settled the disagreement between Section 9 and fundamental rights in Saroj Rani vs. Sudarshan Kumar Chandra.

The Supreme Court upheld the Delhi High Court's decision in [24]***Harvinder Kaur vs. Harvinder Singh (AIR 1984 Delhi HC)*** that "the decree's only purpose was to offer an incentive for the spouses to live together; it does not force an unwilling wife to engage in sexual relationships with the husband."

Restitution is only meant to protect marriage as an institution, and it doesn't go against the ideas in Articles 14, 19, and 21 of the Indian Constitution. The court also said that decreeing

22 - Sourced from AIR Law Journal
23 - Sourced from AIR Law Journal
24 - Sourced from AIR Law Journal

restitution shall not force the partners to have sexual relations, but it ultimately brought them together.

In the law, "consonance" means "the right to be with and be associated with one's spouse."

Recent Case on the Rights of Couples:

The Indian Supreme Court heard a writ case in March 2019 called [25]***Ojaswa Pathak vs. Union of India.*** It questioned whether the restitution of conjugal rights allowed by several family laws, such as section 9 of the Hindu Marriage Act, 1955, was constitutional.

The issue prompted the complaint.

1. This rule takes away a woman's freedom because it forces her to go back to her husband even if she doesn't want to.
2. The law also went against the private interests of men and women who had their own personal freedom.
3. It pushes the partner who doesn't want to have sex with the other person, which is against Articles 14 and 21 of the Indian Constitution.
4. Because it unfairly affects women, it goes against Article 14 and Article 15(1) of the Constitution.
5. The case is still being heard by the Supreme Court's bench of three judges.

[25] - Sourced from AIR Law Journal

CASE HANDLED BY ME:

This is an intriguing case where the husband filed a petition for divorce, but the wife did not accept it. Their marriage was a love-cum arrangement. Both the families were monetarily equal, but their caste and language were different. My client, a lady, faced harsh criticism in her matrimonial home due to her dark complexion and caste. She somehow overcame all those comments, but the husband who had to stand by her gave up on her for silly reasons, which resulted in his filing a divorce case.

My client never gave up her love for him and for the welfare of their son. She filed a counterclaim for restitution of conjugal rights and battled the case for nearly 7 years, and finally her husband joined her and their son. Throughout those seven years, my client encountered numerous challenges, yet her parents provided unwavering support for both her and her son. More than my client, her parents were very curious to make the marriage work and never complained about their son-in-law. They considered him their only son. Hence everyone's prayer and patience in waiting for my client gave a positive result. The bond between them grew stronger than before. Today they are living as a joyful family.

CHAPTER 7

C—CRUELTY AND OTHER GROUNDS FOR DIVORCE

In Hindu society, marriage is seen as a holy bond. Before the Hindu Marriage Act of 1955, there was no allowance for divorce, as it was deemed too extreme for the Indian society of that era. Women were the unseen sufferers under this stringent system. The notion of divorce was not acknowledged, and it was expected that a woman would adapt and compromise. However, with the introduction of the Hindu Marriage Act in 1955, the concept of divorce and corresponding provisions began to evolve to meet the needs of an ever-changing society.

SECTION 13 OF THE HINDU MARRIAGE ACT 1955 SAYS

Divorce— (1) Any marriage solemnized, whether before or after the commencement of this Act, may, on a petition presented by either the husband or the wife, be dissolved by a decree of divorce on the ground that the other party—

1 [(i) has, after the solemnization of the marriage, had voluntary sexual intercourse with any person other than his or her spouse; or

(ia) has, after the solemnization of the marriage, treated the petitioner with cruelty; or

(ib) has deserted the petitioner for a continuous period of

not less than two years immediately preceding the presentation of the petition; or]

(ii) has ceased to be a Hindu by conversion to another religion; or

(iii) has been incurably of unsound mind or has been suffering continuously or intermittently from mental disorder of such a kind and to such an extent that the petitioner cannot reasonably be expected to live with the respondent.

Explanation. — In this clause,

(a) the expression "mental disorder" means mental illness, arrested or incomplete development of mind, psychopathic disorder or any other disorder or disability of mind and includes schizophrenia;

(b) the expression "psychopathic disorder" means a persistent disorder or disability of mind (whether or not including sub—normality of intelligence) which results in abnormally aggressive or seriously irresponsible conduct on the part of the other party, and whether or not it requires or is susceptible to medical treatment; or] 3 * * * **

(v) has 4 * * been suffering from venereal disease in a communicable form; or*

(vi) has renounced the world by entering any religious order; or

(vii) has not been heard of as being alive for a period of seven years or more by those persons who would naturally have heard of it, had that party been alive;

[Explanation. —In this subsection, the expression "desertion" means the desertion of the petitioner by the other party to the marriage without reasonable cause and without the consent or against the wish of such party, and includes the wilful neglect of the petitioner by the other party to the marriage, and its grammatical variations and cognate expressions shall be construed accordingly.]

(1A) Either party to a marriage, whether solemnized before or after the commencement of this Act, may also present a petition for the dissolution of the marriage by a decree of divorce on the ground—

(i) that there has been no resumption of cohabitation as between the parties to the marriage for a period of 9 [one year] or upwards after the passing of a decree for judicial separation in a proceeding to which they were parties; or

(ii) that there has been no restitution of conjugal rights as between the parties to the marriage for a period of 9 [one year] or upwards after the passing of a decree for restitution of conjugal rights in a proceeding to which they were parties.

(2) A wife may also present a petition for the dissolution of her marriage by a decree of divorce on the ground, —

(i) in the case of any marriage solemnized before the commencement of this Act, that the husband had married again before such commencement or that any other wife of the husband married before such commencement was alive at the time of the solemnization of the marriage of the petitioner: Provided that in either case the other wife is alive at the time of the presentation of the petition; or

(ii) that the husband has, since the solemnization of the marriage, been guilty of rape, sodomy or [bestiality; or]

(iii) that in a suit under section 18 of the Hindu Adoptions and Maintenance Act, 1956 (78 of 1956), or in a proceeding under section 125 of the Code of Criminal Procedure, 1973 (2 of 1974) (or under the corresponding section 488 of the Code of Criminal Procedure, 1898 (5 of 1898), a decree or order, as the case may be, has been passed against the husband awarding maintenance to the wife notwithstanding that she was living apart and that since the passing of such decree or order, cohabitation between the parties has not been resumed for one year or upwards;

(iv) that her marriage (whether consummated or not) was solemnized before she attained the age of fifteen years and she has repudiated the marriage after attaining that age but before attaining the age of eighteen years.

Explanation. —This clause applies whether the marriage was solemnized before or after the commencement of the Marriage Laws (Amendment) Act, 1976 (68 of 1976).]

AUTHOR'S EXPLANATION:

In the past, Hindu Dharma Shastra stated that marriage was a holy and unbreakable bond. Prior to the passage of the Hindu Marriage Act in 1955, no laws permitted divorce. The old system was very biased toward men, which is why this act was made. Man can choose how to live his life. He was living a strange life and wasn't being questioned as much.

Section 13 of this Act sets out the grounds for divorce and lets both parties bring their case to a court that can grant a divorce decree. In order for a marriage to end, one partner had to be found guilty of behaviour that seriously hurt the relationship.

The fault-based view of divorce grew out of this change. Even though most people thought of marriage as an eternal union, it became clear that even those kinds of ties could end. However, prior to the enactment of this act, there was a dearth of effective divorce laws.

"Divorce" literally refers to the dissolution of a couple's marriage through legal proceedings.

What are the different ideas about divorce?

1. Theory of Faults:

This idea, which is also called the crime theory or guilt theory, says that a marriage can end when one partner hurts the other and the other partner is found not guilty.This idea says that there is both a guilty and an innocent person in the marriage.

The only person who can get a divorce is the one who is not guilty.

Both sides can't get any help if they are both found to be at fault.

2. The theory of mutual consent:

When both parties choose to get married, they should also be able to divorce freely, with their full consent, and without any fraud, coercion, undue influence, or mischief.

However, this method is strongly criticized for possibly encouraging immorality because it could cause people to get divorced quickly and end their marriages over small personality differences.

However, it is being criticized because it allows people to “LIVE AND LET LIVE” without making things worse. In other words, it speeds up the process and eases the mental pain instantly.

3. The theory of irretrievable breakdown of marriage:

When issues between a married couple get so bad that there is no chance of getting back together, they don’t want to stay together.

These are such extreme and difficult conditions that the couple cannot stay married.

Because of this, the need to live apart is stronger than the love, affection, and loyalty that normally hold a husband and wife together.

We should dissolve a marriage that is unsalvageable, as we cannot salvage a dead marriage.

In the event that a marriage does not survive, there is no reason to keep the shared rights and duties of both parties.

4. Adultery:

That's what Section 13(1)(i) of the Hindu Marriage Act 1955 stated regarding adultery.

Adultery occurs when a married person has a sexual relationship with a non-spouse of the opposite sex, whether married or not.

In a polygamous marriage, having an affair with the first or second wife is not seen as adultery.

Having sex with the second wife is considered adultery, though, if the second marriage is not legal.

Previously, a partner could only receive a divorce if they were continuously living with someone else through adultery. But the Marriage Laws Amendment Act of 1976 changed this so that a single act of adultery could be enough to get a divorce.

It should be legal to be married so that adultery is a crime.

Adultery isn't possible if one person doesn't agree to be involved.

5. Cruelty:

In the Hindu Marriage Act, there are nine grounds why either party can ask for a divorce, and the court can give it. "Cruelty" is one of these reasons, which is listed in Sec. 13(1)(i-a).

Abuse of both the mind and body is considered as cruelty.

These behaviours are affected by partners' lives and places, so each case must be examined individually.

Most of the time, it's easier to understand what physical abuse is than what mental cruelty is.

Persistent effort of the wife to convince the husband to be separate from the family constitutes an "act of cruelty," and the husband is entitled to a decree of divorce.

If the wife sends a reply notice stating that the husband is a drunkard, gambler, womanizer, and pimp. It will amount to mental cruelty.

Repeated threats of suicide are cruel.

The concept of cruelty has varied over the course of time from society to society depending upon the impending social and economic condition of the individual and the society he/she lives in.

Acts like demanding a dowry, refusing to have children, and irretrievably breaking up a marriage have been considered cruel.

Cruelty need not be direct but can also be indirect.

If an individual's conduct is intentionally cruel, it indeed contributes to cruelty.

There are two types of cruelty with reference to intention as an essential characteristic, in one intention is evident, whereas in the other intention is not evident and hidden or absent.

6. Desertion:

The Hindu Marriage Act 1955 has a section 13(ib) that talks about what desertion means.

The respondent is required to cease living with the petitioner voluntarily, without a valid reason, and relinquish all marital rights, duties, and responsibilities. It is clear that if they want to leave the marriage, it will be seen as desertion.

Being away from home for a short time while still talking on the phone or through texts does not count as desertion. The husband and wife should stop having a relationship abruptly.

It is possible to get a divorce if the petitioner has been abandoned by the respondent for two years straight before the case is filed.

7. Conversion:

Section 13(1)(ii) of the Hindu Marriage Act 1955 says what it is.

If either person changed their religion without their partner's permission, the partner who was not converted can go to court and ask for a divorce.

8. Insanity:

Section 13(1)(iii) of the Hindu Marriage Act 1955 defines what insanity means.

The word "insanity" comes from the word "insane," which means having a mind that is not sound or logical.

So, someone who can't tell the difference between right and wrong or who can't give informed consent or make decisions about their own life isn't considered to be able to get married.

People shouldn't expect the petitioner to keep living with the respondent.

9. Venereal Disease:

Section 13(1)(v) of the Hindu Marriage Act 1955 says that it can be a reason for divorce.

Venereal disease, which is also known as a sexually transmitted disease (STD).

The other partner can file for divorce if the sick spouse has a serious, incurable disease that spreads easily.

10. Renunciation:

Section 13(1)(vi) of the Hindu Marriage Act 1955 says that a divorce case can be brought.

If one partner gives up everything materialistic by converting to any religion or another belief system,

As Maslow put it, this individual reaches a state of self-actualization and wants to break free from all ties in the world, even marriage.

One of the main reasons people get divorced is when they no longer want to take care of the duties that come with marriage, relationships, and family.

11. Presumption of Death:

Section 13(1)(vii) of the Hindu Marriage Act 1955 says that presumption of death is a ground for divorce.

A person is thought to be dead if their family or friends haven't heard anything about them being alive or dead for seven years or more.

This is a valid reason for divorce, but the person asking for the divorce is the one who needs to show proof.

Why can a wife get a divorce instead of a husband?

Section 13(2)(i) of the Hindu Marriage Act 1955 says that the wife can file for divorce if the husband has more than one wife.

Section 13(2)(ii) of the Hindu Marriage Act 1955 says that the wife can end the marriage if the husband performed rape, sodomy, or bestiality.

A wife can file for divorce if she gets a maintenance order under Section 125 of the Criminal Procedure Code, 1973, or a decree under Section 18 of the Hindu Adoption and Maintenance Act, 1956, and the couple hasn't lived together again for a year or more.

The wife can get out of the marriage before she turns eighteen if she got married before she was fifteen.

Hindu marriage—A fine observation.

1. Hindu marriage is a sacred and holy union of husband and wife, by virtue of which the wife is completely transplanted to the household of her husband and takes a new birth. It is a combination of bone-to-bone and flesh-to-flesh relationships. To a Hindu wife, her husband is her God, and her life becomes one with him. She demonstrates selfless service and profound dedication to her husband. She not only shares the life and love but also the joys and sorrows, the troubles and tribulations of

her husband and becomes an integral part of her husband's life and activities.

2. [26]Colebrook, in his book 'Digest Hindu Law," described the status of the wife as: "A wife is considered as half of the body of her husband, equally sharing the fruit of pure and impure acts; whether ascending the pile after him or surviving for the benefit of her husband, she is a faithful wife."

3. We only want to remind both the father and mother that they might fight endlessly, but when one person who is sandwiched, disturbed, pained, or shocked, they should always remind themselves that they are parents and not only husband and wife. If the future of the children is kept in mind by both the father and mother, they will think of disposing of all other differences between them.

WHAT DOES NOT AMOUNT TO CRUELTY?

The Supreme Court has consistently made it clear that normal wear and tear between couples will not amount to cruelty. Cruelty should be such that it will make it impractical. The court's request for the couple to continue cohabitation under the current conditions is both political and unreasonable, and the respondent's mere name-calling does not constitute cruelty.

Continued cruel acts by the respondent will not be considered desertion, as she or he was forced to desert because of intolerable behaviour one had to put up with. This situation is also known as constructive desertion. In such a situation, cruelty will not

[26] - Sourced from AIR Law Journal

be considered to be done by the individual who does the act of desertion, but the person who forced the other person to leave him/her will be considered as the one who committed cruelty.

CASE LAWS:

1. The definition of mental cruelty was provided by the Supreme Court in the case of [27]***Trimbak Narayan Bhagwat vs. Smt. Kumudini Trimbak Bagwat [AIR 1967 Bom.80]*** on the victim having the potential to make it practically unfeasible for the victim to continue living with the perpetrator.
2. The Supreme Court in the case of [28]***Samer Gosh vs. Jaya Gosh, 2007 (4) S.C.C.,*** stated that acute mental pain, agony, and suffering would make it impossible for both parties to live together and could come within the parameters of mental cruelty.
3. In the case of [29]***Naveen Kholi vs. Neelu Kholi [AIR 2006 S.C. 2006.S***16.75e Supreme Court observed that the matter complained of should be grave. A a relationship's ups and downs cannot be deemed cruel in a marriage.

Swan vs. Swan, (1953) 2 All ER 854. The facts of that case were as follows: For several periods during their married life, the husband had been a voluntary patient in a mental hospital. During the intervals in which he had returned to the matrimonial home, he had committed acts of cruelty towards his wife. On

[27] - Sourced from AIR Law Journal
[28] - Sourced from AIR Law Journal
[29] - Sourced from AIR Law Journal

the hearing of the wife's petition for divorce on the ground of her husband's cruelty, there was medical evidence which was accepted by the court that at the material times the husband did not know the nature and quality of his acts.

It was held, "In these circumstances, the husband was not capable of being guilty of cruelty to the wife."

The House of Lords has explained the position in two recent decisions. In ***Gollins v. Gollins, (1963) 2 All ER 966 and Williams vs. Williams, (1963) 2 All ER 994,*** the question arose as to whether the husband would be held guilty of cruelty when he was not deliberately treating the wife with cruelty and in fact was oblivious of the consequences of his actions upon his spouse. The ruling concluded as follows:

Though one partner must want to hurt the other for it to be cruel as a matrimonial offense, it is material and may be crucial."

The House of Lords further held:

"Whether cruelty, as a matrimonial offense, has been established is a question of fact and degree, which should be determined by taking into account the particular individuals concerned and the particular circumstances of the case, rather than by any objective standard; accordingly, in situations where both partners are mentally and physically healthy and the respondent's behaviour is so bad that the other partner shouldn't have to put up with it, cruelty has been proven. It doesn't matter what the respondent was thinking; it's cruel whether the respondent's behaviour was "aimed at" the other partner or just because they didn't care, which could be because they were selfish or lazy.

In a verdict passed by the Rajasthan High Court in [30]***Neetu vs. Vinod, dated 21 February 2025, in Civil Miscellaneous Appeal No. 1239/2024,*** divorce on the grounds of mental cruelty was decreed in favour of the husband based on the fact that there was an irretrievable breakdown of marriage. The false allegation made by the wife for dowry, etc., has been overcome by the husband by proving that the wife has left her husband and lived separately for five years without physical relations; her actions are categorized as cruelty towards the husband. A wife's prolonged separation from her husband with the intention of living apart and without any physical relation constitutes cruelty under matrimonial law. The wife's failure to provide evidence of dowry demands, her intention to live separately, and her consistent blackmailing of the husband indicates a lack of reconciliation in their relationship. Additionally, the previous false allegation of dowry demands further submission is the claim of cruelty. The court found no illegality or infirmity in the impugned order, leading to the dismissal of the appeal for lack of merit.

In a verdict passed by the Karnataka High Court in [31]***Anupama vs. Sri N.Y. dated 22 November 2024 in MFA No. 202306/2024,*** divorce on the grounds of cruelty was ordered in favour of the husband. He fought against false allegations of illicit relationships made by his wife. The wife's allegations were baseless, such as illicit relationship, defamation, and bigamy against the husband,

30 - Sourced from indiakannon.org
31 - Sourced from indiakannon.org

without any proof, which eventually affected his character and service. Despite mediation, the wife's conduct and defamatory statements indicate that she is not willing to reconcile. The trial court pointedly observed that if the wife were really intended to live, she would not have made all such baseless allegations against the husband. She would have preferred a petition for restitution of conjugal rights. Hence, the intent of the wife was not to live; the Hon'ble court was pleased to dismiss the appeal filed by the wife.

The verdict passed by the Supreme Court Judgement - Laws (TLNG)-2025-1-28.

Hindu Marriage Act 1958 Sections 13 (1) (i-a) and (III). The petitioner stated that the respondent constantly avoided intimacy, which meant that they could not have a conjugal relationship. The couple has not lived together since 2013 and their marriage is no longer together. The long time apart and the respondent's behaviour have hurt the petitioner's mental health, making living together unpleasant. Due to the current situation, reconciliation is neither possible nor useful for restoring marital unity. There has been no marital togetherness over the years, which shows that the marriage is over and can't be fixed. The respondent's lack of concern has caused the petitioner a lot of emotional pain, which supports the claim of mental abuse even more. A marriage that hasn't grown or changed in over ten years can't be brought back to life. The long-lasting estrangement shows how pointless it is to keep the legal connection going. Based on the information, the High Court decided that the marriage had lost its meaning and essence. Because of this, the civil general appeal was granted, and the marriage ended.

The verdict passed by the Bombay High Court 0n 20th February 2025 in a Second Appeal No. 268/2018.

Hindu Marriage Act, 1955-Section 13-Civil Procedure Code, 1908-Section 100-Dissolution of marriage - Mental Cruelty -Decreed in favour of the husband-Appeal against the same by wife. The husband has not only stated that his wife threatened to kill themselves and put him and his family in jail, but it was actually attempted by her. The husband substantiated allegations of cruelty through cogent testimony of multiple witnesses. The wife made unsubstantiated allegations against the husband's father without filing any police complaint. Such conduct constitutes mental cruelty sufficient to warrant dissolution of marriage under matrimonial law. No perversity in the trial court's findings of fact regarding cruel treatment-Appeal is dismissed.

CASE HANDLED BY ME:

This case has been pending for nearly 8 years, with the other party's intention being to harass my client. It was actually a love-cum-arranged marriage. Both are professionals and have a favourable societal status. Education should elevate one's thoughts and actions, but in today's world, education primarily focuses on paper, not on action and behaviour.

The world preaches only money. The other side is solely focused on money, driven by emotions such as anger, avarice, greed, arrogance, and jealousy. These traits have destroyed the family structure, causing it to fall apart. The misunderstanding and other qualities are the main reason for the separation of this couple.

Family and relationship understanding are the foundation of a fulfilling married life. When the foundation is weak, then no matter how classy the building looks, it will fall down in a small breeze. Likewise, this family setup was also disturbed by these qualities. And finally ended up filing a divorce case on the grounds that there were allegations of cruelty against my client.

The son was trying to take advantage of the situation. This illustrates the challenges faced by single parents. This was the second round of litigation between the parties. My client was patient enough to tolerate the other side's atrocity. Finally, the grounds were proved by us, and we have gotten the verdict in favour of my client.

CHAPTER 8

E- EXTENDING PROTECTION FOR VOID AND VOIDABLE MARRIAGES

Void Marriage:

Section 11: Void marriages—Any marriage solemnized after the commencement of this Act shall be null and void and may, on a petition presented by either party thereto against the other party, be so declared by a decree of nullity if it contravenes any one of the conditions specified in clauses (i), (iv) and (v) of Section 5.

AUTHOR'S EXPLANATION:

Any marriage that takes place after this law goes into effect is null and void, and either party can file a petition with the court against the other party. If any of the conditions specified in Section 5 clauses (i), (iv), or (v) are violated, the marriage is declared null and void.

There are rules about null and void marriages in Section 11 of the Hindu Marriage Act. The Hindu Marriage Act does not define a "void marriage," but it does provide an explanation for why a marriage might not be valid.

Under the Marriage Act, a marriage is not valid if it doesn't meet the requirements set out in section 5 clauses (i), (iv), and (v).

1. The Section 5 clause says that neither person had a spouse living at the time of the marriage.
2. According to Clause (iv) of Section 5, both parties are not in a prohibited relationship unless the tradition or usage that governs each of them allows them to get married.
3. Clause (v) of Section 5 states that both parties are not sapindas of each other unless their respective customs or usages allow them to get married.

What does it mean for a marriage to be void or voidable?

1. To be void means that something is not valid or it has no legal effects.
2. A void marriage is not valid from the beginning and is usually viewed the same way by the law as if it never happened.
3. The Hindu Marriage Act, 1955, stipulates that a marriage must meet certain conditions to be considered legal. Failure to meet these conditions renders the marriage either null and void or subject to nullification. If they are not met, the marriage is either null and void or can be made null and void.

When is a marriage declared void?

1. Another spouse who was living with them at the time of the marriage. When you marry someone else while you are officially married to another, this is called bigamy.
2. The degree of relationship that is not allowed. According to Section 3(g) of the Hindu Marriage Act, the following describe

two parties who are in a relationship that is not allowed.

If one is the lineal ascendant of the other; or

If one was married to a lineal descendant or ascendant of the other; or

If one was married to the other's brother, father's or mother's brother, or grandfather's or grandmother's brother; or

If they are a brother and sister, an uncle and niece, an aunt and nephew, or the children of a brother and sister or two brothers and sisters,

3. Section 5(iv) of the Hindu Marriage Act states that a marriage between both parties who are in a prohibited relationship that is against the law is void. It also states that a marriage is legal if it is validated by the customs or habits of both parties involved.

4. According to Section 18(b) of the Hindu Marriage Act, parties who get married in a way that breaks the law can be punished for up to one month or fined up to Rs. 1000/-, or both.

5. "Sapinda" means the term "by Hindu law" is used.

Sapinda to the same ancestor; this is called a sapinda connection. When two people are related through blood, they are said to be sapinda.

A Sapinda relationship renders a person's marriage null and void.

6. As per Section 3(f) of the Hindu Marriage Act, sapinda is defined as follows:

A person's relationship with another person goes back to

the third generation (inclusive) through the mother and the fifth generation (inclusive) through the father. We trace the line upwards from the individual in question, who represents the first generation.

If one or both of two people have a lineal ascendant within the limits of a sapinda relationship, they are sapindas of each other.

7. Section 5(v) of the Hindu Marriage Act states that a marriage that takes place in a sapinda is void. It also asserts that the customs or practices of both parties involved make a marriage legal.

"Void Marriage": What Does It Mean?

1. Both parties don't have the status of husband and wife in a void marriage.
2. Section 16 of the Hindu Marriage Act states that children born from a void marriage are legitimate.

VOIDABLE MARRIAGES

Section 12. Voidable marriages — (1) Any marriage solemnized, whether before or after the commencement of this Act, shall be voidable and may be annulled by a decree of nullity on any of the following grounds, namely:

[(a) that the marriage has not been consummated owing to the impotence of the respondent; or]

(b) that the marriage is in contravention of the condition

specified in clause (ii) of section 5; or

(c) that the consent of the petitioner, or where the consent of the guardian in marriage of the petitioner [was required under section 5 as it stood immediately before the commencement of the Child Marriage Restraint (Amendment) Act, 1978 (2 of 1978)], the consent of such guardian was obtained by force [or by fraud as to the nature of the ceremony or as to any material fact or circumstances concerning the respondent]; or

(d) that the respondent was at the time of the marriage pregnant by some person other than the petitioner.

(2) Notwithstanding anything contained in sub-section (1), no petition for annulling a marriage—

(a) on the ground specified in clause (c) of sub-section (1) shall be entertained if—

(i) the petition is presented more than one year after the force had ceased to operate or, as the case may be, the fraud had been discovered; or

(ii) the petitioner has, with his or her full consent, lived with the other party to the marriage as husband or wife after the force had ceased to operate or, as the case may be, the fraud had been discovered;

(b) on the ground specified in clause (d) of sub-section (1) shall be entertained unless the court is satisfied—

(i) that the petitioner was at the time of the marriage ignorant of the facts alleged;

(ii) that proceedings have been instituted in the case of a

marriage solemnized before the commencement of this Act within one year of such commencement and in the case of marriages solemnized after such commencement within one year from the date of the marriage; and

(iii) that marital intercourse with the consent of the petitioner has not taken place since the discovery by the petitioner of the existence of [the said ground].

AUTHOR'S EXPLANATION:

If a marriage is performed before or after this law goes into effect, it can be ruled voidable by a court verdict of nullity if any of the following are true: the respondent was unable to have children; the marriage violates the conditions set out in clause (ii) of section 5; the petitioner's consent was forced or obtained through fraud about the nature of the ceremony or any important facts or circumstances about the respondent; or the respondent was pregnant by someone other than the petitioner at the time of the marriage.

No matter what else is said, a petition to end a marriage according to consent will not be considered if it is submitted more than one year after the force had stopped working or the fraud had been discovered or if the petitioner lived with the other party to the marriage as husband or wife after the force had stopped working or the fraud had been discovered.

The grounds listed shall be accepted unless the court is satisfied that the petitioner did not know about the facts alleged at the time of the marriage and that proceedings have been initiated within one year of a marriage occurring before the commencement of this Act and within one year of a marriage occurring after the commencement of this Act and that the petitioner has not had sexual relations with another person with their permission since discovering the existence of the said ground.

Here are some ways that void and voidable marriages are different:

VOID MARRIAGES	VOIDABLE MARRIAGES
The marriage In other words, it is void from the very beginning. ie Void Abnitio	Any of the parties involved can choose to end the marriage, or it can be valid if both agree to it.
A decree is the only thing that a court of law can say about a marriage being void.	Through a decree of nullity, the court of law ends the marriage.
It is legal for them to get married again without first getting a Decree of Nullity from thecourt.	They can't get married again until the first one is annulled by a court order called a "Decree of Nullity."
In a marriage that is void, the wife does not have the right to maintenance.	A wife in a marriage that is voidable can ask for maintenance.
The parties do not hold a status of husband and wife in a void marriage.	The parties hold a status of husband and wife in a voidable marriage.

CASE LAWS:

1. In [32]***Lily Thomas v. Union of India, the Supreme Court*** said that a second marriage will be considered void if a Hindu spouse changes his religion in order to marry someone else, but not because he wants to practice that faith. A part of the Indian Constitution, Article 21, is also violated.

2. In the case of [33]***Smt. Yamuna Bai v. Anant Rao, the Supreme Court*** said that a woman who is married for the second time is not really a wife because the marriage was void from the beginning, and she cannot ask for maintenance under Section 125 of the Code of Criminal Procedure, 1973.

3. The Supreme Court ruled in [34]***Revan Siddappa vs. Mallikarjun (2023)*** that a child born from a marriage that was not valid or was not voidable has the right to a share of their parents' Hindu Undivided Family (HUF) property under the Mitakshara law.

It was made clear, though, that such However, it should be noted that a child born into a Hindu Undivided Family (HUF) does not automatically become a co-parcener as any rights or duties toward the other.

4. In [35]***Lila vs. Laxman,*** it was decided that a void marriage doesn't need a declaration of nullity. In the view of the law, it's not a marriage. A court order for void marriage is just a statement that the marriage does not exist. It is a fact that the court said that both parties are not married.

32 - Sourced from indiakannon.org
33 - Sourced from indiakannon.org
34 - Sourced from indiakannon.org
35 - Sourced from indiakannon.org

5. In the case [36]***C.S. Rangabhattar vs. C. Soodamani,*** it was decided that a husband who cohabits with his wife cannot ask for the marriage to be void, even knowing a fact before marriage that she is pregnant.
6. In [37]***Sarabai vs. Komalsingh,*** the court heard the case after eight years of marriage. The court decided that the plea was too late and could not be considered. The court dismissed it.
7. In the case of [38]***Monia Khosla vs. Amardeep Khosla,*** the husband wasn't able to connect with women because he wasn't interested in them, and he also didn't have sex with his wife. Because of this, the court said that his wife should be able to get a ruling that the marriage is null and void because they haven't lived together formally, as their marriage was not consummated.

CASE HANDLED BY ME:

These types of cases are very common filing before the court. In this case both were studying in college. Both the families were equally rich but different religions. Both felt there is no scope of the parents to accept the marriage. Hence the other party by undue influence somehow convinced the girl to get the marriage registered and also registered the same.

When the girl's family came to know the fact, they were not ready to accept the same and they agitated the same. The girl side approached me to get their marriage dissolved on the

[36] - Sourced from indiakannon.org
[37] - Sourced from indiakannon.org
[38] - Sourced from indiakannon.org

grounds of nullity. Here the consent of the girl was obtained by undue influence and it was within one year she had come for the proceedings I was able to file the case and got a decree of Nullity of marriage.

CHAPTER 9

An overview of the Hindu Marriage Act and Conciliation

HINDU MARRIAGE ACT 1956

SECTION 2: Act Applies to

1. Hindus, including Virashaiva, a Lingayat, or a follower of the Brahmo, Prarthana, or Arya Samaj,
2. Buddhists, Jains, or Sikhs.

SECTION 3: Deals with Definitions

1. Customs and usage signify a rule followed for a long time.
2. District court, principal civil court of original jurisdiction.
3. Full blood and half blood.
4. Full blood: descendants of a common ancestor but with the same wife.
5. Half-blood: descendants of a common ancestor with a different wife.
6. Uterine blood: descendants of a common ancestor from a different husband.
7. Prescribed: means prescribed by the rules.
8. Sapinda Relationship: third-generation relation.
9. If one is a lineal descendant of the other.

10. Degrees of prohibited relationships.

SECTION 4:

Overriding Effect of this Act

SECTION 5: Conditions of Hindu Marriage.

1. Neither party has a spouse living at the time of marriage.
2. Is incapable of giving valid consent due to unsoundness of mind.
3. Suffering from mental disorder.
4. Suffering from insanity.
5. Bride groom completed 21 years old and the bride 18 years old at the time of marriage.
6. Parties are not within degrees of a prohibited relationship.
7. Parties are not sapindas, but if custom permits, it is not a bar.

SECTION 7: Ceremonies for a Hindu Marriage

1. May be solemnized with the customary rites and ceremonies of either party.
2. Taking Saptapadi (seven steps) by parties before sacred fire, marriage is completed.

SECTION 8: Registration of Hindu Marriage

RESTITUTION OF CONJUGAL RIGHTS AND JUDICIAL SEPARATION

SECTION 9: Restitution of Conjugal Rights.

1. When either party without an aggrieved party may seek restitution of conjugal rights.
2. Reasonable cause to live separately is on the party who states also.

SECTION 10: Judicial Separation

1. Either party can seek judicial separation on the grounds in section 13(1), and a wife can also seek relief on the grounds of 13(2).
2. The court can rescind the degree of application by a party.

NULLITY OF MARRIAGE AND DIVORCE

SECTION 11: Void Marriage

Marriage can be declared void if it contravenes clause(i) (iv) (v) of section 5.

SECTION 12: Voidable Marriage

1. Marriage may be annulled by a decree of nullity if:

a. Marriage has not been consummated.

b. Contravenes section 5(ii).

c. Consent of the guardian obtained by force.

d. Respondent was pregnant at the time of marriage by some other person.

2. No petition for annulling a marriage—

a. (i) No petition can be made after one year.

(ii) The petitioner lived with the consent of the other party.

If the petitioner was ignorant of the pregnancy, the petition cannot be entertained.

(ii) Proceedings were initiated one year after the act came into force.

(iii) the marital intercourse with the consent of the petitioner not taken place.

SECTION 13: Divorce

Marriage can be dissolved by a degree of divorce on the following grounds:

1. Had voluntary sexual intercourse with any other person than the spouse
2. Treated the petitioner with cruelty
3. Deserted petitioner for a continuous period of 2 years preceding that date of petition.
4. Ceased to be Hindu by conversion.
5. An unsound mind or mental disorder by a petitioner cannot be expected to live.

6. Suffering from venereal disease.

7. Has renounced the world.

8. Has not been heard from for 7 years.

13 (1A) Divorce can be asked for on the following grounds also:

i. No resumption of cohabitation for one year after the decree of judicial separation,

ii. No restitution of conjugal rights for one year after the said decree.

13 (2) A wife may also present a petition for the following grounds:

1. Husband is married.
2. Husband is guilty of rape, sodomy and bestiality.
3. Maintenance granted under section 18 of the Hindu Marriage Act, under section 128 of the CRPC, and no cohabitation for one year after the decree or order.
4. That marriage is solemnized before 15 years of age and repudiated before 18 years of age.

SECTION 13-A: Alternate Relief in Divorce Proceedings.

Except in petitions under clause (ii)(iv) and (vii) of subsection (1) of section 13, courts can pass a decree for judicial separation.

SECTION 13-B: Divorce by Mutual Consent

1. Both parties can file the petition on the ground.
2. They have not been able to live together.
3. They have mutually agreed that the marriage should be dissolved.

4. Not earlier than 6 months from the date of petition and before 18 months, after enquiry parties, a decree can be passed.

SECTION 14

(1) No petition for divorce within one year of marriage. If the respondent committed exceptional hardship or depravity, the petition can be filed.

(2) In any such seeking permission to file before a 1-year court to consider interests of children and reasonable probability of reconciliation.

Section 15: When can a divorced person marry again?

After decree of divorce if there is no appeal or right to appeal and if appeal time expires without any appeal being filed, either party can marry again.

SECTION 16: Legitimacy of children of void and voidable marriage

1. Any child of such marriage shall be legitimate.
2. Even a child born to parties with respect to voidable marriage is legitimate.
3. The child gets rights to the property of the parents.

SECTION 17: Punishment of bigamy

Punishable under sections 394 and 495 of the IPC.

Section 18: Punishment for contravention of other conditions for a Hindu marriage. Contravention (iii), (iv), and (vi) of section 5 shall be punishable.

a. If contravention of clause (iii)—simple imprisonment for 15 days or a fine extending to Rs. 1000 or both.

b. If contravention of clause (iv) or (v)—simple imprisonment for 1 month or a fine extending to Rs. 1000 or both.

SECTION 19: Court to which petition shall be presented

To be presented to the district court without the whole ordinary original civil jurisdiction

i. The marriage was solemnized.

ii. Respondent resides at the time of filing of petition.

iii. Parties last resided together.

iii(a) if the wife is the petitioner where she is residing on the date of presentation of the petition.

iv. Petitioner resides where Respondent resides in territories outside to which this Act extends and has not been heard off for more than 7 years.

Section 20: Contents and verification of the petition

1. The petition should state that there is no collusion between the parties.

Verify statements in writing and use them as evidence at the hearing (SECTION 21).

All proceedings are regulated by CPC.

Section 21A: Power to transfer petitions

This section states that two petitions are presented in 2 different courts; later petitions should be transferred to the court where the first petition was verified.

Section 21B: Special provision relating to the trial and disposal of petitions under the Act

The trial will continue day by day.

ii. The Trial to be expeditious and concluded within 6 months from the date of service of notice.

iii. Ever the respondent must receive notice of each appeal within 3 months.

SECTION 21C: Documentary evidence

No document shall be inadmissible in evidence on the ground that it is not duly stamped or registered.

SECTION 22: Proceedings are to be in camera and may not be printed or published.

i. Proceedings are to be in camera and may not be printed or published.

ii. **If the person violates the law, they will face a** fine of Rs.

1000/-.

SECTION 23 Decree in proceedings

1. If the court is satisfied
2. Petitioner is not taking advantage of his or her wrong; if petitioner is filed under clause (i) of subsection (1) of section 13, the petitioner has not confined or condoned the acts complained of or the act of cruelty. (bb). mutual consent.
3. The petitioner did not present themselves in collusion; there was no use of force, fraud, or undue influence to obtain the consent.
4. Improper delay in presenting the petition.
5. There is no other legal ground to refuse the relief.
6. The court shall decree such relief accordingly.
   a. Before granting any relief, the court makes every endeavour to effect conciliation between the parties.
   b. To effect conciliation, refer the matter to any person named by the parties or to anyone nominated by the court.
   c. When the court passes a divorce decree, it must provide each party with a free copy of it.

Section 23A: Relief for respondents in divorce and other proceedings

In any proceedings under the act, the respondent may not only approve but may make a counter-claim to any relief under the act, and the court can grant it.

SECTION 24: Maintenance and expenses of proceedings.

1. Pending proceedings, either wife or husband with no independent income can apply for monthly maintenance and expenses for the proceedings.
2. The respondent must receive the aid petition within 60 days from the date of notice service.

SECTION 25 Permanent Alimony and Maintenance.

1. Either party can claim maintenance as a gross sum or on a monthly basis, and the court can grant it by creating a charge on the respondent's immovable property.
2. Yes, for either party, in that instance of either party, it can be varied, modified, or rescinded.
3. If the party to whom the alimony is granted has remarried or in case the wife has not remained chaste, or in case the husband has had sexual intercourse with any other women outside wedlock, the court can vary, modify or rescind the order.

SECTION 26: Custody of children.

1. Courts can pass orders regarding the custody, maintenance, and education of minor children and from time-to-time revoke, suspend, or vary any such orders.
2. The application shall be disposed of within 60 days from the date of service of notice on the respondent.

SECTION 27: Disposed of property

A decree can provide for the disposal of the property presented at or about the time of marriage belonging jointly to both.

SECTION 28: Appeals from decree and order.

1. Appealable as a decree of court to be presented to the court to which ordinary appeal lies.
2. Orders under section 25 and section 26 are appealable if they are not interim orders.
3. No appeal lies regarding costs.
4. Appeal to be preferred within 90 days from the date of decree or order.

SECTION 28: Enforcement of decree and order.

Can be executed like civil court decrees.

SECTION 29: Savings:

1. Marriages before this act are valid.
2. Rights recognized by custom will not be affected by the Act.
3. Pending proceedings on the date of the act are valid.
4. Provisions do not affect the Special Marriage Act, 1954.

CERTAIN SPECIAL FEATURES OF THE ACT TO BE NOTED

1. Normally pleadings will not be evidence unless Section 20(2) says that the petitioner or another qualified person must verify the information in every petition under this Act in the same way that complaints are verified by law. The hearing may use the statements in the petition as evidence. Section 21A deals with cases that undergo transfer.

2. Section 21A, Transfer of cases if two OP's between the parties are pending in two different courts; the petition filed later is to be transferred to the court where the earlier petition was filed.

3. Documents, if not duly stamped or registered However, under Section 21C, they are admissible.

4. Jurisdiction, now after the amendment on 23.12.2003 states that if the wife is the petitioner, the place of her residence will give jurisdiction to the court.

5. FREE COPY OF DECREE: A copy of the decree of divorce shall be given free of court to each of the parties as per section 23(4).

6. The respondent can seek the relief which he could have otherwise claimed by means of a separate petition.

7. If the husband has no independent income, he can also claim interim maintenance against the wife. This is allowed under section 24.

8. Section 23-A: In same petition seeking Restitution or Judicial Separation or Divorce, the Respondent while contesting the same, can counter-claim any relief under the Act and the

Court may grant the same which he or she would have been entitled to if he or she presented a petition seeking such relief on that ground.

9. Section 13- B: Non mentioning of reason for separation. It has been held in AIR 2016 Mad 165 and also referred in AIR 2021 Bombay 33 that Court cannot deny divorce to parties, after being convinced that parties cannot live together and they opted to dissolve marriage peacefully. Court should not investigate into reason of separation and decide if parties are justified to live separately or not, under section 13-B. Decree of Divorce by mutual consent must be granted. One year separation is mandatory.

TABULAR COLUMN FOR OTHER ACTS OF PERSONAL LAWS.

Acts	Mutual consent	Maintenance-Interim and Permanent Alimony	Visitation Rights	Judicial Separation	Restitution conjugal Rights	Grounds for divorce	Null and Void Marriages	Voidable Marriages	Conciliation
THE SPECIAL MARRIAGE ACT, 1954	Section 28	Section 36, Section 37	Section 38	Section 23	Section 22	Section 27	Section 24	Section 25	Section 34(2), 34(3).
THE PARSI MARRIAGE AND DIVORCE ACT, 1936	Section 32-B	Section 39, Section 40	Section 49	Section 34	Section 36	Section 32	Section 30	-	-
THE DIVORCE ACT, 1869	Section 10-A	Section 36, Section 37	Section 41	Section 23	Section 32	Section 10	Section 18	-	-
THE HINDU MARRIAGE ACT, 1955	Section 13-B	Section 24, Section 25	Section 26	Section 10	Section 9	Section 13	Section 11	Section 12	Section 23(2) 23(3)

CONCILIATION IS THE PRIMARY OBJECT OF THE MARRIAGE ACTS.

What is conciliation?

- The primary object of the marriage acts is the conciliation process.
- This is an alternative approach to settling disagreements that can settle a lot of big disagreements quickly and cheaply.
- When it comes to family disputes, conciliation as an alternative dispute resolution method will be very helpful. India has the Family Courts Act, 1984, which lets us use conciliation to settle our family disputes in a fair and appropriate way.
- Family courts try to settle disagreements through mediation and settling for the following personal laws:

1. There are six parts in the Family Courts Act, and Section 23 talks about conciliation. In Section 9, it says that the family court has to try to reach a settlement.
2. Two sections of the Hindu Marriage Act, 23(2) and 23(3), talk about conciliation in marriage.
3. Sections 34(2) and 34(3) of the Special Marriage Act deal with conciliation.
4. According to the Quran, there are four steps that must be taken to make a Muslim marriage work before the Talaq is given.

The first step is that if there is a marriage dispute, the husband has to try to talk about the differences with the wife and sort out the issues. The Quran refers to this as Faizuhunna.

The second step is that the parties to the marriage should be asked to stay temporarily separate, and there should be no physical relationship that may help them reunite. The Quran calls this practice Wahjuruhunna.

The third step is for the husband to discuss the seriousness of the situation with the wife, promote reconciliation, and do his best to make the marriage work. This step may also fail. The Quran refers to this as Wazribuhunna.

In the fourth step, if the disagreement is still not resolved, the Quran says that it must be brought before two arbitrators who are family members of each partner. These are the four steps that the Quran tells Muslims to follow to make peace.

The 129th Report from the Law Commission says that judges should be required to find other ways to settle disagreements once the issues have been set. Any of these alternative methods to settle disagreements can lead to a settlement: arbitration, mediation, conciliation, judicial settlement, or Lok Adalat. We apply this strategy in civil conflicts.

WHY IS CONCILIATION MANDATORY?

Marriage involves many small details, such as food habits, family culture, sleeping patterns, self-care, discipline, different living arrangements, and adaptability. These terms need a lot of understanding; they should have some people skills in them. In a marriage relationship, the mind will work, and the heart will stay quiet.

The marriage institution is full of emotions and relationship bondage. Moreover, in India, people belong to different religions and beliefs. They are governed by different personal laws in respect of the matter relating to family, i.e., marriage, divorce, inheritance, etc. In all personal laws, conciliation is mandatory.

The main object and aim of the conciliation and reconciliation is to support and motivate couples to resolve their problems, strengthening their relationship, family bondage, preserving the culture of the family, children's welfare, understanding the heritage of our country, and emphasizing that unity is always strength. The by-product is a happy society with great values, good citizens, and a developed country in the world strategy.

The children brought up in broken families lack the emotional support of the parents, taking advantage of the situations, easily being trapped by the fake relationship, getting into all sorts of harmful habits and bad company. There are exceptions to this, too. The percentage ratio is higher when compared to the organized family setup. We know youngsters are the hope for tomorrow's society.

Conciliation helps preserve the marriage rather than resorting to divorce. All the family laws include the provisions of mediation, conciliation, and counselling sessions even before they start the case.

Case Laws:

1. The Division Bench of the Calcutta High Court stated in [39]***Shiv Kumar Gupta v. Lakshmi Devi Gupta, 2005 (1) HLR 483*** that it is the job of the judge in marriage cases to follow Section 23(2) of the Hindu Marriage Act, 1955.

2. In the case of [40]***Jagraj Singh v. Bir Pal Kaur, JT 2007 (3) SC 389,*** the Supreme Court said the following:

   "The Hindu Marriage Act, 1955" is a special act that deals with marriages, restitution of conjugal rights, judicial separation, and marriages and divorces that are not valid. Chapter V (Sections 19–28A) deals with the court's power and how to go about filing a motion for restitution of conjugal rights, judicial separation, or divorce. Subsection (1) of Section 23 makes it evident that when a petition for divorce is made under Section 13 of the Act for certain reasons, the court must attempt to bring the parties back together "in the first instance" before granting any relief.

3. [41]***Salem Bar Association v. Union of India (2003 (1) SCC 49)*** is the case where the Supreme Court provided the final version of the Model Rules of ADR and the Model Rules of Mediation. All high courts in the country were directed to accept these rules with any modifications that were necessary.

[39] - Sourced from indiakannon.org
[40] - Sourced from indiakannon.org
[41] - Sourced from indiakannon.org

PRE-LITIGATION COUNSELLING:

Generally, when matrimonial clients approach us, we will first understand their mindset. Then we shall suggest what the legal parameters available are for sorting out their issues. Then, we will suggest to them some previous cases that have been handled, as well as the court's procedure, the time duration, and other practical difficulties. At this point in time, some of the clients will open up and vent about their issues.

Only the concerned parties may participate in the counselling session. Hence the client will feel free to open up. I shall allow them to talk and shall not intervene in between. Mostly there will be no big issues. During the question-and-answer session, some insight will open up for them. Many clients have changed their decisions and tried to cope with matrimonial life, and they have thanked me for their happy lives.

Recently, one of my clients rejoined her husband. She has a kid. Considering the welfare of the kid and her life, she rejoined the matrimonial life and now lives happily. In her case, cash handling was the only issue. Once they resolved that issue, they were able to unite.

In another case, during the conciliation session, both husband and wife came together. Both of them never uttered a single complaint against each other. They loved each other and burdened each other. During the session, they comprehended each other's pain points, gained clarity, and joyfully left my office.

Nowadays, due to the financial freedom of both men and women, they feel their privacy should not be disturbed, and they both have to share household work equally for the smooth functioning of the family. These are all meagre issues which can be solved easily. And most of them are in the nuclear family setup. So they lack the elders' support. Some of the couples see elders as a blessing and some as a burden. Couples who see them as a blessing escape from the big loss of losing their life. Those who perceive them as a burden may find it difficult to manage even minor issues, ultimately leading to the loss of their precious life.

I generally don't advise the clients; I just give them some suggestions and guidance on how they can find solutions for their problems. The impulsive state of mind will not allow them to think of solutions. They will always focus on problems. I will just tell them to take a small dimension shift so that they can lead a joyful life. If my clients are in the reading habit, I shall suggest some books like:

1. "Hold Me Tight: Seven Conversations for a Lifetime of Love" by Dr. Sue Johnson.
2. "The Seven Principles for Making Marriage Work" by John Gottman.
3. "Mating in Captivity: Unlocking Erotic Intelligence" by Esther Perel.
4. "His Needs, Her Needs: Building an Affair-Proof Marriage" by Willard F. Harley Jr.
5. "The Five Love Languages" by Gary Chapman.
6. "Men are from Mars and Women are from Venus" by John Gray.

The only thing is that the couples must understand that

"CHANGE IS CONSTANT." For this, at least one partner should be aware of these facts. They will understand when to bend and when to remain straight. My dear readers, kindly understand that life is all about learning new lessons every day. Think of your partner as the most exceptional person in the world. Enjoy the differences in each other's character; give enough time to understand each other. In my experience it will at least take a minimum of 5 years for proper understanding. The bond will form from the very beginning. You must have the patience to take it forward.

If you keep yourself busy with your work and allot sufficient time for personal space for your partner, you will experience a fulfilled and meaningful life. Marriage not only gives you companionship but also a best friend where you can be yourself and not change your originality; you can express your thoughts without any hesitations, exactly like a shoulder to share your burden and love. Hence, do not lose this relationship for flimsy reasons.

CASE HANDLED BY ME:

This is a very peculiar case. Both parties are natives of Bangalore, and it was an arranged marriage for them. The marriage took place in Chennai, where both parties resided and worked in the IT industry. Both the parties loved and understood each other well. Their familial pride compelled them to submit a divorce petition to the court. Both of them stated that, for the benefit of the family, they would file a petition for mutual consent to divorce, as the parties' family members require the divorce verdict to be documented in writing.

Their question to me was if we remarry again, will this court decree be a bar for them to get their marriage registered? I said law does not prohibit it. After they obtained the divorce decree, they sent the court verdict to their respective families to satisfy their ego.

The biggest twist is that, after receiving a divorce decree, they remarried, officially registered their marriage, and settled in the USA. The parties here wanted to live together. Hence no court or family can stop them from being together and living a joyful life. Even if you obtain a divorce decree, no court will stop you from getting married again with the same partner. This was way back in the year 2010.

AUTHOR'S EXPLANATION:

It was really a different experience for me in my practicing career when I handled this case. I really felt worthwhile in conducting their case. They were also law-abiding citizens. Hence, they too wanted to perform their marriage legally. The piece of advice given to them helped them rejoin their matrimonial lives. The intent of the parties was that "now we don't have children, but in the future, after we are together without marriage, they will be termed as illegitimate children, and my wife will be termed a concubine. This pathetic situation should not come to my future generation." Given the circumstances, I supported them until they remarried and departed for the USA.

In this case, I encountered the unpleasant faces of both

families and socially responsible couples who aspired to live with dignity for themselves and the future generation of society.

From this case I wish to convey to my readers that life is too short to fight, curb, take revenge, be cruel, express hate, ego, sadistic pleasure, etc.; instead, respect the life partner, treat them with dignity, enhance the love and understanding, trust each other, not let a third person in your personal issues, not condemn, correct, criticize, or compare in public, etc., for living a meaningful life by accepting all the differences of each other.

Conclusion:

The matrimonial disputes are very sensitive issues. The parties involved in the dispute would reach court with various family statuses. The court guarantees that any party approaching the family court must mandatorily attend the three counseling sessions, even before the other side replies to the case filed. Hence, the courts are very mindful that the parties have free space to express their problems and seek a solution.

If the parties cannot reach a settlement, they return to the regular court to contest their case. The court also liberally grants adjournments to the parties so that there can be enough time to reconcile their decisions for the welfare of the family setup. The judicial system works utmost for the welfare of the parties involved in the disputes. In matrimonial cases, the courts extend their time until they pass a verdict.

SUGGESTIONS:

Native Indians are traditional and don't like to consult outside experts and counsellors. India has a lot of people, so it's suggested that more people learn about how useful alternative dispute resolution systems can be in the Indian culture.

In our court system, there is a program called "Free Legal Aid." To achieve this, we need to set up more camps in our country's remote villages and explain the benefits of the process. In this manner, we can resolve the majority of disputes at the local level.

Additionally, family courts should be empowered to help more people. There should be more family courts all over the country so that family issues can be settled more quickly.

AUTHOR'S EXPERIENCE:

I am a true believer in the words, **"INSPIRING AND IMPACTING LIVES."** Even as a child, luminaries in all fields, including spiritual gurus, inspired me. Life is full of learning and unlearning. Learning will be about maturing in the thought process and progress of life, and unlearning will be the removal of unwanted beliefs and habits inside us. This is how human lives evolve. Let us align ourselves with the path of nature, lead meaningful lives, and assist both mankind and the creatures of nature.

The matrimonial society is a Heart and Soul game. The strain in a relationship is not the only consequence of loss. **Health, wealth, and the most valuable resource, "TIME," all have**

a connection with it. Most importantly, we all have finite time to stay in this world. **We, the human species, should have the logical mindset to use the finite time for an infinite joyful life.** If you are a joyful human being, you can do wonders, magic, and miracles in life.

Hence, I have titled this book as "**DIVORCE IS EXPENSIVE"** with the able guidance of my guruji, Shri Murali Sundaram. There is a long quest inside me to say to my fellow mankind: don't harm and punish yourself by getting yourself separated from a marital relationship for fragile reasons, because living is a bigger picture with all sorts of emotions—love, war, dance, and all masala in it. Every movie is different. So, understand the storyline of your life and paint your picture with trust, love, compassion, understanding, adjustment, etc.

With the above insights, I finish this book with Gratitude

CHAPTER 10
Formats

Maintenance Petition

IN THE COURT OF THE

I.A.No. / 20…

in

H.M.O.P. No. …

Mrs. xxxxxxxxxx,

D/o…………,

Residing at

…Petitioner/Respondent

-vs-

Mr. xxxxxxxxxxx,

S/o…………………,

Residing at

...Respondent/Petitioner

AFFIDAVIT OF

I, ………………, aged …… years, W/o. ……………., D/o. ………………………… Residing at do hereby solemnly affirm and sincerely state as follows:

1. I am the Respondent in the above OP, and the Petitioner herein. I am conversant with the facts of the case.
2. I submit that the Petitioner has filed the above OP seeking divorce against me on the grounds of cruelty and desertion. I submit the main petition may be read as part and parcel of this affidavit.
3. I submit that the Respondent/Petitioner was working as a clerk in ....and in the year .... he was earning nearly .... per month. And now the Respondent/Petitioner would be earning more than forty thousand per month. I submit that because of the Petitioner I lost my peace and all the earnings and savings. Hence the Petitioner is liable to maintain my son .... Already my aged mother has no source of independent income; hence, it is very difficult for her to maintain herself. Now I and my son have become another burden for her.
4. I submit that the Respondent/Petitioner is solely responsible to maintain me and my son after marriage. Even the ATM card was under his custody. Hence the Respondent/Petitioner is duty-bound to maintain me and my son. I submit the Respondent/Petitioner has sufficient income to maintain me and my son. Hence as a dutiful husband, he has to maintain me and my son. He is duty-bound to pay the school fees, which run about Rs. ..../- every year, and other curricular expenses for my son.
5. I submit that it is clearly seen that the Respondent/Petitioner

was never of moral or financial support to me or my son. I submit that after marriage I have given all my salary and savings to him only. The Respondent /Petitioner considered me and my son for his social status and as a money vending machine. The constant and object neglect and not rendering conjugal duties caused severe mental cruelty to me.

6. I submit that I had undergone a lot of mental agony and cruelty from the Respondent/Petitioner throughout my matrimonial life. I had made maximum efforts to make this marriage work, but the Respondent / Petitioner has only responded to my efforts with indifference, cruelty, and verbal abuse. The Respondent/Petitioner has not paid the school fees from .... The arrears of school fees stand at ..../- (......................). I submit that I have borrowed money from my brothers for paying the school fees. Since the Respondent/Petitioner is a duty-bound father, he has to repay the loans incurred for the educational expenses of our only son.

7. I therefore pray that this hon'ble court may be pleased to direct the Respondent/Petitioner to pay a sum of Rs. ..../- each month towards the interim maintenance for my son .... the arrears of school fees of Rs. ..../- and Rs................./- towards the litigation expenses to me and thus render justice.

Solemnly affirmed and signed Before Me

this at Chennai on

IN THE COURT OF THE

I.A.No. / 20…

in

H.M.O.P. No. ………..

Mrs. xxxxxxxxxx,

D/o………………..,

Residing at

…Petitioner/Respondent

-vs-

Mr. xxxxxxxxxxx,

S/o...................,

Residing at

...Respondent/Petitioner

PETITION FILED UNDER SECTION 24 OF HINDU MARRIAGE ACT 1955

For the reasons stated in the accompanying affidavit it is therefore respectfully prayed that this Hon'ble court may be pleased to pass an order to direct the Respondent/Petitioner to pay a sum of Rs. ..../- each month towards the interim maintenance and the arrears of school fees of Rs............./- and Rs......../- towards the litigation expenses to the Petitioner's/Respondent's son .... and thus render justice.

Dated at Chennai on this the ...... day of ....

Counsel for Petitioner/Respondent.

Mutual Petition

IN THE COURT OF THE

H.M.O.P. No. of 202..

XXXXXXX

D/o.,

W/o.,

Residing at

...1st Petitioner.

And

XXXXX

S/o.,

Residing at

...2nd Petitioner.

PETITION FILED UNDER SECTION 13-B OF HINDU MARRIAGE ACT 1955

1. The 1st Petitioner is XXXXXXX, aged about ...... years, D/o.......... and W/o. ...., Hindu, residing at .... Within the jurisdiction of this Hon'ble court.

2. The 2nd Petitioner is XXXXXXX, aged about ...... years, S/o. ...., Hindu, residing at ....

   The address for service for both the Petitioners are that of their counsel, ..., having office at ....

3. The marriage between the 1st and 2nd Petitioners were solemnized as per Hindu, rites and customs on .... at .... and the Marriage was Registered on .... at Registrar .... in Registration No. .... No children were born out of the marriage. After the marriage, both the Petitioners were residing together as husband and wife at ....

4. Due to incompatibility of temperament between the 1st and 2nd Petitioners, both have not been able to lead a happy life and are both discontent with one another and do not perceive the possibility of living together in peace. Despite efforts from elders, friends and relatives, the marriage between them has irretrievably broken down. Considering the widening chasm between them, they have decided to part amicably. There has been no cohabitation between them.

5. Both the Petitioners have understood and appreciated the inaptness they have for one Another is realizing that their relationship cannot be patched up and that they cannot put up with it. one another and live together, they have decided to part amicably. Hence the 1st and 2nd Petitioners have come forward to seek dissolution of marriage on the ground of mutual incompatibility.

6. Both the Petitioners have exchanged all articles and have no claim whatsoever against each other in respect of movable and immovable properties of the other, in any manner for the past, present or future.

7. Both the Petitioners have waived their right to maintenance and/or alimony—past, present and future and have no claim

whatsoever against each other in movable and/or immovable properties.

8. Both parties agree and undertake that both of them shall relinquish any and all rights that he or she may hereafter acquire to act as executor or administrator of the estate of the other party. It is the intention of both the parties that their respective estates/properties shall be administered and distributed in all respects as though no marriage has been solemnized between them.

9. Both parties represent and warrant to each other that neither of them has contracted any debts, charges or liabilities whatsoever and is not in possession of any document or endorsement, and in case there is any document or other endorsement or any other thing for which either of them, personally or their property, shall be or become liable or answerable, both parties covenant to each other that they will at all times keep each other free, harmless, and indemnified against and from any and all debts and liabilities heretofore or hereafter contracted or incurred by either of them because of such document or otherwise.

10. Both the parties submit they undertake not to interfere in each other's lives in any manner whatsoever. Both the parties further undertake not to make any allegation in the future, either by themselves or through their friends, relatives, agents, servants, or assigns, or through any other person, against each other in the future and not to interfere in their private lives in any manner, including dissemination of information in any form through social

media like WhatsApp, Twitter, Facebook, or Instagram, etc.

11. Both parties declare not to claim any share of movable or immovable properties possessed or owned at present or that they may acquire in the future against each other.

12. Neither party has any further claim against the other on any other score.

13. The Petitioners submit that they have filed this petition out of their own free will and volition. They also submit that this petition has not been filed under any duress, fraud, coercion, force, or undue influence and that there is no collusion between them.

14. The Petitioners herein submit that the cause of action for the above O.P. arose at .... within the jurisdiction of this Hon'ble Court when the 1st Petitioner herein, living at ...., developed un-patchable differences on .... when they were last separated, and as they continue to live separately for over .... The 1st Petitioner is now residing well within the jurisdiction of this Hon'ble Court.

15. The Petitioners herein submit that the above O.P. is incapable of valuation and pay a fixed court fee of Rs. /- under Art. I Sch. II of the TNSV & CF Act, 1955.

16. The Petitioners therefore pray that this Hon'ble Court may be pleased to grant a Judgment and Decree of divorce

dissolving their marriage on the grounds of mutual consent, which was solemnized as per Hindu, rites and customs on .... at .... and the Marriage was Registered on .... at the Registrar of .... in Registration No. ...., and pass such further or other orders as this Hon'ble Court may deem fit and proper and thus render justice.

Dated at .... on this the .... day of ....202...

Counsel for Petitioners I Petitioner

II Petitioner

VERIFICATION

We, the Petitioners herein do hereby declare that the contents stated above are true to the best of our knowledge, belief and information.

Dated at .... on this the .... day of .... 202......

Counsel for Petitioners I Petitioner.

II Petitioner

STATEMENT OF ADDRESS OF THE PARTIES UNDER ORDER VI RULE 14-A OF CPC

I Petitioner:

XXXXXXX

D/o.,

W/o.,

Residing at

And

II Petitioner:

XXXXX

S/o.,

Residing at,

The Address for service for both the Petitioners is that of their counsel …………………… having office at No. ………………..

Dated at ……………. on this the …….. day of ………….. 202..

Counsel for Petitioners I Petitioner.

II Petitioner.

VERIFICATION

We, the Petitioners herein do hereby declare that the contents stated above are true to the best of our knowledge, belief and information.

Dated at .... on this the ....day of ....202...

I Petitioner.

II Petitioner.

DOCUMENTS FILED ALONG WITH THE PETITION UNDER ORDER VII

RULE 14(I) of CPC

1. Marriage Registration Certificate (Photocopy)
2. Marriage Invitation (Original)
3. Marriage Photo (Original)
4. Aadhar Card of the 1st Petitioner (Photocopy)
5. Aadhar Card of the 2ndPetitioner (Photocopy)

Dated at .... on this the .... day of .... 202....

Counsel for Petitioners I Petitioner

II Petitioner

VERIFICATION

We, the Petitioners herein do hereby declare that the contents stated above are true to the best of our knowledge, belief and information.

Dated at .... on this the ....day of ....202....

I Petitioner

II Petitioner

Cruelty

IN THE COURT OF THE

……………………………………………………………………

H.M.O.P.No. / 20…….

Mrs. xxxxxxxxxx,

W/o………………….,

Residing at

...Petitioner

-vs-

Mr. xxxxxxxxxxxx,

S/o……………………,

Residing at

...Respondent

PETITION FILED UNDER SECTION 13(1)(i-a) OF HINDU MARRIAGE ACT 1955

The Petitioner above named submits as follows:

1. The Petitioner above named is the wife of ………………., Hindu, aged about ……….. years, residing at …………………………

   The address for service is as stated above.

2. The Respondent above named is the son of

.............., Hindu, aged about ...... years, residing at ....

The address for service is as stated above.

3. The Petitioner submits that she and the Respondent were working in a private concern at .... They both fell in love and their love was not accepted by their respective parents. So the Petitioner came out from her house and both the Petitioner and the Respondent went to .... and got their marriage registered as per the Hindu Marriage Act 1955 on .... solemnized at .... before the Registrar of Marriages at .... in Serial No..................... Through the wedlock, the Petitioner and the Respondent were blessed with a girl/boy child namely .... now aged .... yrs. Since it was a love marriage and a registered marriage, no pictures were taken at the time of marriage only joint photos are available.

4. The Petitioner submits that after their marriage, both the Petitioner and the Respondent were staying in his parents' house for a few years. There the Petitioner has suffered immensely. The Petitioner submits that the behaviour of the Respondent and his parents was not accommodative. The Respondent also never supported the Petitioner at any point in time when his parents were troubling her. The Respondent also used to drink and come every day. Because of that, also, the Petitioner suffered at most there. Moreover, the Respondent used to get money from strangers and he will not repay it promptly. Because of this, the Petitioner was put into

severe mental agony.

5. The Petitioner submits that they were blessed with a girl/boy child. Then after .... the Petitioner and the Respondent went separately and began their matrimonial house. While they were staying separately, the Respondent used to drink every day and used to hurt the Petitioner. Some days the Respondent used to drink at the house also. Because of this attitude of the Respondent, me and my child were affected both physically and mentally. More than this, his abusive language injured the Petitioner and the kid more. The Petitioner submits that the kid was not able to concentrate on her studies either. The mental and physical abuses were undergone by the Petitioner and the child. This suffering could not be measured or put into words.

6. The Petitioner submits that the Respondent will not go to work properly, and he will not give any money for the daily expenses. Because of this many days, the Petitioner and her child suffered a lot without food also. The Petitioner's and the kid's health were very much affected. The Petitioner submits that his old habit of borrowing money from strangers also continues now. Every day it was a nightmare for the Petitioner because the moneylenders used to abuse the Petitioner with filthy language. But the Respondent never cared about these issues. Even finally after the Respondent left the matrimonial house on .... the Petitioner was informed by the house owner .... and the next house member .... that the Respondent had borrowed money from them, which this Petitioner was not aware of.

The Petitioner was put under severe mental pressure and was totally depleted of all her energy. Since the Petitioner was left alone with the girl child, she was totally shattered, with all her confidence and mental strength gone. Then the Petitioner decided to vacate the house. At that time there was a great shock and surprise waiting for the Petitioner that is, the house owner never allowed the Petitioner and the child to vacate the house without clearing the dues. Then at last the Petitioner's mother and well-wisher came and rescued the Petitioner and the kid. In spite of it, the house owner took the sofa, air conditioner, and bike of the Respondent; the next house member took the television. Then finally the Petitioner took the asylum with the aged mother of the Petitioner in the above-stated address. Then the Petitioner gave a complaint before the .... police station on .... till date the Respondent has not been able to be traced out by the police officials.

7. The Petitioner submits that the marriage of the Petitioner with the Respondent has been a miserable failure and the Petitioner holds the

Respondent and his family are wholly and exclusively responsible for the same. The Respondent is the erring spouse and he and his family had tortured the Petitioner excessively. The Petitioner and her daughter were left in the lurch with no resources to even sustain themselves. They took shelter at the residence of her aged mother, the Petitioner at ....

8. The Petitioner states that she and her daughter, since .... when they were abandoned by the

Respondent, started living with the aged mother of the Petitioner. The Respondent has shut down by absconding till date all his legal and moral obligations towards his wife and child.

9. The Petitioner submits that her living is supported by her mother. The Petitioner has been living in her shadow, and she has burdened her aged mother exceedingly. The Petitioner's aged mother, on the other hand, has her own family to cater to, and the Petitioner living with them weighs down on her financially. Despite their struggling financial situation, the Petitioner's aged mother has large-heartedly taken care of the Petitioner and her daughter and provided them with basic sustenance.

10. The Respondent has absconded from all obligations towards the Petitioner and is splurging his earnings upon himself. The Petitioner is suffering to make ends meet and traumatized by the very thought of being a burden on the Petitioner's mother.

11. The Petitioner's future turned meaningless. The Petitioner married the Respondent under the belief that her life partner would be an emotional and financial support for her; the Respondent has dumped her in every walk of her life. The attitude of the Respondent reveals that he does not have a soft corner for the Petitioner and her daughter.

12. The Respondent has not fulfilled any of his obligations either as a husband or a father and has left the Petitioner in the lurch. The Petitioner submits that the Respondent's attitude reveals that he has wanted to walk away from his

obligation and is disinterested in sorting out the issues between the Petitioner and the Respondent. The Petitioner states that as a direct consequence of the treatment meted out to her, she has suffered physically and emotionally. The Petitioner is physically weak and mentally stressed.

13. The Petitioner submits that she lost all hope of a successful marriage following such events. The Respondent insulted her in public places and has been very generous with invectives. The Respondent's attitude and behaviour are irreparable and the Respondent is very content living his own life culling off the Petitioner from it. The Respondent's disappearances have multiplied and the Petitioner have worn out beyond my stamina to convince the Respondent to lead a normal life.

14. However, the Respondent seemed to have different plans in mind. The Respondent's needs are way beyond the reach and ability. The Petitioner has lost all hope in the Respondent and it has been proven to the Petitioner beyond doubt that the Respondent married the Petitioner only for a financial source of income and to lead a luxurious life. The Petitioner has suffered immensely and been humiliated beyond illustration.

15. The Petitioner is frustrated and not willing to condone his cruelties any further. The Petitioner does not want her only daughter to witness such dramatic and unpleasant scenes, which might naturally affect their education and the Petitioner therefore forced to file a petition for divorce on the grounds of cruelty.

16. The cause of action for this petition arose on the date of marriage between the Petitioner and the Respondent as per the Hindu Marriage Act on .... solemnized at ...., before the Registrar of Marriages at .... in Serial No. .... Her only daughter was born, and the Respondent deserted the Petitioner and his daughter from the year .... and on several dates when the Respondent committed severe cruelties upon the Petitioner as stated earlier and where the place of marriage is within the jurisdiction of this Hon'ble Court.

17. The Petitioner submits that there is no collusion between the Petitioner and the Respondent in filing the above Petition, and the Petitioner has not condoned the cruelty and the irretrievable loss of matrimonial life.

18. The Petitioner had paid a sum of Rs......../- as and towards the court fee under Article I and Schedule 2 of the Tamil Nadu Courts Fees and Suits Valuation Act 1955.

19. Therefore, it is respectfully prayed that this Hon'ble Court may be pleased to pass an order of Decree and Judgment

i. of divorce by dissolving the marriage solemnized between the Petitioner and the Respondent as per the Hindu Marriage Act on .... solemnized at No..............................., before the Registrar of Marriages at .... in Serial No............... on the grounds of Cruelty,

ii. And pass such further or other orders as this Hon'ble Court may deem fit and proper in the circumstances of the case and thus render justice.

Dated at …………… on this the ….. day of ……………..

Petitioner.

VERIFICATION

I, the Petitioner herein do hereby declare and verify that all that has been stated by me in the above paragraphs 1-19 is true to the best of my knowledge, belief and information.

Verified at …………….. on this the ……… day of …………………

Petitioner

LIST OF DOCUMENTS

1. Marriage Registration Certificate (Photocopy)
2. Joint Photo (Original)
3. Residence proof of Petitioner (photocopy)
4. Birth Certificate of the Daughter/Son (Photocopy)

Petitioner

VERIFICATION

I, the Petitioner herein do hereby declare and verify that all that has been stated by me in the above paragraphs is true to the best of my knowledge, belief and information.

Verified at .... on this the .... day of ....

Petitioner

LIST OF DOCUMENTS FILED UNDER ORDER VII RULE 14 (2) OF C.P.C.

Nil at Present

Dated at .... this the .... day of ....

Petitioner

STATEMENT OF ADDRESSES UNDER ORDER VII RULE 14 (1) OF CPC.

Petitioner: xxxxxxxxxxxxx,

W/o..................,

Residing at,

Respondent: xxxxxxxxxxxxx,

S/o.....................,

Residing at,

Petitioner

VERIFICATION

I, the Petitioner do hereby declare that the facts stated by me in the above paragraphs are true to the best of my knowledge, belief and information.

Verified at .... on this the .... day of ....

Petitioner.

Advance the Hearing For Mutual Petition

IN THE COURT OF………………………

I.A. No. of 20…..

IN

H.M.O.P. No. of 20…

xxxxxxxxxxx,

W/o. ……………….,

Residing at

… I Petitioner.

And

xxxxxxxxxxxxxx,

S/o……………………,

Residing at

… II Petitioner.

AFFIDAVIT OF

I, ..., aged about ...... years, S/o. ...., Hindu, residing at ...., do solemnly affirm and state as follows:

1. I state that I am the Petitioner herein and 2nd Petitioner in the above OP and as such, well aware of the facts of the case. I am filing this affidavit and petition on behalf of the 1st Petitioner also. The main petition may be read as part and parcel of this affidavit.
2. I submit that the above petition has been filed by me and the 1st Petitioner for dissolution of marriage as per Hindu rites and customs and the marriage was solemnized on .... at .... The marriage was Registered before the Sub Registrar of on .... Out of wedlock, we are not blessed with any child.
3. I submit that I am residing in Mumbai and employed in Norway. Now, with great difficulty, I have come down to Chennai only to appear before this Hon'ble court to give evidence in the above O.P. I am on the verge of losing my job in Norway. Risking my job security, I wanted to put an end to my matrimonial issue. I am unable to continue with this dead marriage, which causes huge mental depression and agony.
4. Unless the above O.P. is advanced today for giving my evidence, I will be put to much hardship, and irreparable loss could happen to me by prejudicing my employment.
5. In view of the Hon'ble Supreme Court in AMARDEEP SINGH -Vs- HARVEEN KAUR - (2017) 8 SCC 746, the statutory

waiting period of six months can be waived when there is no possibility of parties resuming cohabitation and there are no chances of alternative rehabilitation. The waiver application can be filed 1 week after the 1st motion, giving reasons for the prayer for waiver. As we want to move forward in our lives, the statutory waiting period of six months may be waived. I submit the case is posted for hearing on .... I submit that in the interest of justice the hearing in the above case be advanced from .... to this date for the purpose of waiving the waiting period of six months. Otherwise we both shall be facing severe hardships. The facts and circumstances of the case for waiving the statutory period of 6 months have been explained in detail in the waiver application filed along with the instant application.

6. I submit that the mutual consent divorce petition numbered as OP No..............., the case is posted for final hearing on .... Since we have no other issues pending between me and the 1st Petitioner, hence I am filing a waiver petition and an advance hearing petition so as to enable us to file a proof affidavit.

7. I therefore pray that this Hon'ble court may be pleased to advance the hearing of the above O.P. from .... to today or to the earliest day that this Hon'ble Court deems fit and proper in the circumstances of the case so as to enable us to file the proof affidavits in the above O.P. and thus render justice.

Solemnly affirmed and signed Before me

His name in my presence on

This .... day of ....

Advocate, ...

IN THE COURT OF

...

I.A. No. of 20.....

IN

H.M.O.P. No. of 20......

xxxxxxxxxxxxx,

D/o. ....,

W/o.........................,

Residing at

... I Petitioner.

And

xxxxxxxxxxxxx,

S/o. ....,

Residing at

... II Petitioner.

PETITION FILED UNDER SECTION 28(2) OF C.R.P.

For the reasons stated in the accompanying affidavit it is therefore prayed that this Hon'ble court may be pleased to advance the hearing of the above O.P. from .... to today or to the earliest day that this Hon'ble Court deems fit and proper in the circumstances of the case so as to enable us to file the proof affidavits in the above O.P. and thus render justice.

Dated this at .... on ....

Counsel of Petitioner/II Petitioner

WAIVER PETITION FOR MUTUAL

IN THE COURT OF ....

I.A.No. of 20......

IN

H.M.O.P.No......... of 20...

XXXXXXX,

W/o. ....,

Residing at

... I Petitioner.

And

XXXXXXXX,

S/o. ....,

Residing at

... II Petitioner.

AFFIDAVIT OF

I, ..., aged about .... years, S/o. ...., Hindu, residing at ...., do solemnly affirm and state as follows:

1. I am the Petitioner herein and the 2nd Petitioner in the main O.P. the main petition may be read as part and parcel of this affidavit. I am conversant with the facts of the case. I file this affidavit on behalf of the 1st Petitioner also.
2. I submit that both of us and our respective family members decided to dissolve the marriage by filing mutual consent

without any rancor. Accordingly the Petition for Divorce by Mutual Consent has been filed on .... and the same is pending before the ....Court, ... in O.P. No. ....

3. I submit that we were not in terms in the matrimony, and our matrimonial problem was compounded because of serious differences of opinion between us, which culminated in separation, and we have not been living together since ...., and we have been living separately for the past one year and two months. The conciliatory efforts initiated to bring about family union have not fructified, as the matrimonial dispute between us has gone beyond repair. There is no possibility for us to reconcile and reside together, and the marriage is a mere shell, out of which the substance has gone.
4. I submit that both of us, as well as the elders of our respective families, have decided to put an end to the matrimonial dispute in order to avoid tortuous legal proceedings through a court of law. In accordance with the advice, we and our respective family members have resolved to dissolve the matrimonial relationship by filing by mutual consent for dissolving the marriage.
5. I submit that the matrimonial bond has been broken down and there is no chance for a reunion, and we have agreed to put an end to the matrimony. All efforts for mediation/conciliation, including efforts in terms of section 9 of the Family Courts Act to reunite the parties by the Hon'ble Court, have failed, and there is no likelihood of success in that direction by any

further efforts.

6. I submit that in the above context, the waiting period of six months will only prolong our agony. Therefore, the waiting period of six months may be waived in accordance with the latest pronouncement of law by the Hon'ble Supreme Court in AMARDEEP SINGH -Vs- HARVEEN KAUR - (2017) 8 SCC 746, wherein it is observed that **the object of the Court is not to perpetuate a purposeless marriage or prolong the agony of the parties when there was no chance of reconciliation.**

7. I therefore pray that this Hon'ble Court may be pleased to waive the statutory waiting period of six months and to take the case at once so as to submit our evidence in the main petition of divorce by mutual consent and thus render justice.

*

Solemnly affirmed at BEFORE ME

on this the .... day of ....20.........

and signed their name in my presence.

IN THE COURT OF ....

I.A.No. of 20……

IN

H.M.O.P.No……… of 20…

XXXXXXX,

W/o. ……………,

Residing at

… I Petitioner.

And

XXXXXXXX,

S/o. ……………….,

Residing at

… II Petitioner.

PETITION FOR WAIVER FILED UNDER SECTION 151 C.P.C.

For the reasons stated in the accompanying affidavit, it is therefore prayed that this Hon'ble Court may be pleased to waive the statutory waiting period of six months and to take the case at once so as to submit our evidence in the main petition of divorce by Mutual Consent and thus render justice.

Dated at ………..on this the day of ………… 20………

Counsel for I Petitioner/II Petitioner

VISITATION RIGHTS

BEFORE THE HON'BLE ....

I.A.No. of 20....

in

H.M.O.P. No. of 20....

XXXXX

S/o.

Residing at

.... Petitioner/Petitioner

-Vs-

XXXXX

W/o.

Residing at

...Respondent/Respondent

AFFIDAVIT OF

I, XXXX, son of ...., Hindu, aged about .... years, residing at ...., do hereby solemnly affirm and sincerely state as follows:

1. I am the Petitioner herein and the Petitioner in the main HMOP also. I crave leave of this Hon'ble Court to treat the main petition as part and parcel of this affidavit.
2. I state that the Respondent is my wife, and out of wedlock with the Respondent, a son was born to us on ...., and we named him ...., and a daughter was born on

…………., and we named her …………….. My son is now aged about …… years and studying in …. standard at ……………. and our daughter is now aged about …… years and studying in …. standard at ………….. Both are minors and are under the custody of the Respondent/mother.

2. I state that after many turbulences, I was living happily in my own house at ………………………., with our two children, the Respondent and aged mother. The Respondent treated my mother cruelly and chased her out of the house and fought with me that I should not allow my mother inside our house. Though as the only son I am duty-bound to maintain and take care of my mother, for the sake of living with my children, I shifted Mother to another house.

3. The Respondent too purchased a flat out of her income in the next street at ……………. and made her parents live in that house, enabling them to visit our house every day. Due to the intervention of the Respondent's parents, minor issues between us were blown out of proportion, and we are living separately from …………..

4. The Respondent, with a view to preventing me from coming home and seeing my children, on ……………, filed a false complaint before the All Women Police Station at …………… as well as before the ……………….. Police Station, alleging that I attempted to murder her. The sub-inspector of police called me for inquiry and warned me not to go to my house again, even to see my children and further threatened that if I go to my house, I would be arrested. Thus, the Respondent, with the support of police, restrained me from going to my

own house and seeing my children. I am staying away from my house and children until today, apprehending police action.

5. The Respondent then filed a petition for maintenance in ...... before the Judicial Magistrate at .... and several other petitions under The Protection of Women from Domestic Violence Act, 2005, and restrained me from entering into my own house and prevented me from seeing my children. In order to see my children, I voluntarily made monthly payments without even waiting for any order from the court. Despite my gesture to reunite with my children, the Respondent refused to let me meet them. The stubborn and adamant attitude of the Respondent kept the children away from me and caused very unhappy moments.

6. As a father, I wanted my two children to be with me, considering their well-being, too. Therefore, tolerating all the humiliation subjected to me by the Respondent in the court, I always requested her to permit me to visit the children. The Respondent exploited my longing to meet the children and kept demanding more and more money. I always reiterated to the Respondent that the welfare of my children only is of paramount importance to me and assured them that I would bear all the expenses of my children even without any court order, be it education or enjoyment, but the Respondent did not trust me and is giving evasive replies about being with my children. I state that several times I expressed my willingness to join her for the sake of living with my children, but the Respondent refused, stating that she is not interested, without caring about the welfare of the children.

7. After much persuasion, I succeeded in meeting my two children last month, as my daughter had a school function and wanted my presence. Despite the children showing an interest in living with me, the Respondent is neither allowing me to visit them regularly without her consent nor agreeing to a reunion. By not withdrawing any of the cases filed against me, the Respondent is indicating that her intention is not to live together and deprive me from living with my children too.

8. I state that as a father, I am entitled to visit my children. I need not be at the mercy of the Respondent to meet my children and shower love and affection on them. I have a legal right to visit them and I want to exercise my legal right as a father. I am a software engineer placed at Chennai and can take care of the children if interim custody is granted to me. I do care for the happiness of my two children and want to visit them on weekends without disturbing their studies and other routines. I have been separated from my children for more than 3 years, and unless this Hon'ble Court permits me to visit my children every Saturday and Sunday between 9 am and 6 pm at my house where they presently live and permits me to take them out during this time, I will be put to irreparable loss and mental agony.

For the abovesaid reasons, I pray that this Hon'ble Court may be pleased to permit me to visit my son, ……… aged about …….. years, and daughter, aged about 6 years, on every Saturday and Sunday between 9 am and 6 pm at my house where they presently live, and permit me to take them out during this time pending disposal of the main petition and pass such further or other order as deemed fit and proper and render justice.

Solemnly affirmed and signed

his name on this, the 27th day of BEFORE ME

April, 2022 in my presence

ADVOCATE,........................

BEFORE THE HON'BLE ....

I.A.No. of 20....

in

H.M.O.P. No. of 20....

XXXXX

S/o.

Residing at

.... Petitioner/Petitioner

-Vs-

XXXXX

W/o.

Residing at

...Respondent/Respondent

PETITION FOR VISITING RIGHTS U/S 26 OF HINDU MARRIAGES ACT 1955

For the reasons stated in the accompanying affidavit, it is prayed that this Hon'ble Court may be pleased to permit the Petitioner to visit his son, ... aged about ...... years, and daughter, ..., aged about 6 years, on every Saturday and Sunday between 9 am and 6 pm at their house where they presently live and permit the Petitioner to take his children out during this time pending disposal of the main petition and pass such further or other order as deemed fit and proper and render justice.

Dated at ....on this the ....day of ....

Counsel for Petitioner

About the Author and the Book:

Hailing from a distinguished family renowned for its strong values, the author is extremely passionate about her profession. She embarked on her legal journey in the year 2000 at the District Court and enhanced her expertise under the guidance of the esteemed Government Pleader, Shri P.S. Jagannathan. Her extensive experience in the legal field has now transformed her to become an Author, aiming to illuminate the authenticity of the judiciary and how litigants secure their rightful reliefs before the courts.

Married in 2007 to Mr. B.N. Perumal Raja and blessed with a son, Master R. Sai Sanjay, she has dedicated over 25 years to the quest of law and justice more particularly in matrimonial disputes. Having successfully resolved hundreds of such cases, she is widely recognized for her expertise in negotiation and arbitration, ensuring swift and effective resolutions. Her approach is pragmatic—when a marriage is irretrievably broken, she prioritizes efficiency, often concluding mutual consent divorces without unnecessary delays.

A firm believer in client-centric advocacy, she first lends a patient ear before meticulously educating clients on their legal remedies. With this book, she brings forth her vast experience to serve as a guiding light for couples navigating litigation and for young advocates stepping into the legal profession. Through her insights, readers will gain a deeper understanding of the workings of the judiciary and the pathways available to resolve disputes with clarity and confidence.

Made in the USA
Monee, IL
08 November 2026

67973271R00111